Laboratory Manual for

Exercise Physiology

for Health, Fitness, and Performance

Second Edition

Sharon A. Plowman, Ph.D.
Northern Illinois University

Denise L. Smith, Ph.D.
Skidmore College

Thomas E. Ball, Ph.D.
DePauw University

Benjamin Cummings

San Francisco Boston New York
Cape Town Hong Kong London Madrid Mexico City
Montreal Munich Paris Singapore Sydney Tokyo Toronto

Publisher: Daryl Fox
Acquisitions Editor: Deirdre McGill
Project Editor: Susan Teahan
Publishing Assistant: Michelle Cadden
Cover Designer: Kathleen Cunningham
Marketing Manager: Sandra Lindelof
Manufacturing Buyer: Stacey Weinberger

Benjamin Cummings

ISBN 0-321-10658-X

2 3 4 5 6 7 8 9 10—DPC—06 05 04 03 02
www.aw.com/bc

Table of Contents

Contents		Page

Preface

This manual is specifically written to be used in conjunction with *Exercise Physiology for Health, Fitness and Performance* (2nd ed.) by Plowman and Smith, but it is also suited to any Exercise Physiology undergraduate course or laboratory course. We believe that meaningful laboratory experiences are essential to understanding the complex concepts of Exercise Physiology, and that lab is often the most interesting part of an Exercise Physiology course. Because facilities to conduct such labs vary greatly from one institution to another, this manual is designed to provide flexibility to accommodate different laboratory facilities, different class sizes, different instructor preferences and different teaching objectives. This manual is intended to provide this flexibility while still providing the core material that is necessary for any Exercise Physiology course.

Throughout the text, the student is introduced to field tests for assessing physiological function as well as laboratory tests that are the basis for the field tests.

FEATURES:

This manual has a number of features designed to maximize the effectiveness of laboratory experiences as teaching tools for students.

1. Consistent Structure. This manual employs a consistent structure from one lab exercise to another to facilitate student understanding of instructor expectations and to decrease the time necessary to explain each lab. Each laboratory includes:
   - Student Learning Objectives
   - Equipment List (often with options)
   - Procedures
   - Protocols
   - Data Sheets
   - Student Activities: Definitions (key terms), Analysis, Interpretation and Discussion, and Application
   - Related Readings

2. Flexibility. The laboratories in this manual have options to allow the instructor flexibility in modifying the lab exercises for the needs of the particular class size and available equipment.
   - Each laboratory permits the instructor a number of choices to meet the needs of a particular class.
   - There are several labs for each unit, some using laboratory based criterion tests and some using field tests of various measures. Instructors can select appropriate labs for the individual course objectives and available equipment.
   - Most labs contain alternative procedures so that the instructor may select a procedure most appropriate to that class; for example, many labs contain procedures for testing all of the subjects in the class, or for testing only a sample from the class.
   - Each lab has a variety of questions for the students to answer. The manual provides interpretation and application questions at the end of each lab. The instructor can assign some or all of the questions, or he/she can add other questions.

3. Helpful Hints. The manual contains information about how to complete each laboratory, including instructions on construction of scattergrams, line graphs and bar graphs.

4. Reference and Related Materials. *Appendix B* contains a list of journals that publish research in exercise physiology and textbooks that can be used as references.

5. Profile Charts. *Appendix A* contains normative values for as many tests as possible. These allow students to individually evaluate their performances.

6. Projects. *Appendix D* contains options for semester projects which integrate information from several laboratories. These projects are designed to facilitate understanding of basic concepts and practical applications and can be used in addition to or in place of the student activities.

ACKNOWLEDGEMENTS:

We like to acknowledge and profoundly thank Tim Manning for the many, sometimes frustrating and seemingly endless, hours spent typing the manuscript and improving the presentation of the material. In addition, we are grateful to John Vargas for setting up the original template. We would also like to thank the many students on whom we tested and refined many of the labs, as well as the graduate assistant lab instructors throughout the years for their feedback and suggestions.

Sharon A. Plowman
Denise L. Smith
Thomas E. Ball

Informed Consent

As part of this laboratory experience, I understand that I will be asked to perform various tests that are used to demonstrate selected physiological concepts or measure physical fitness. I understand that these tests will be administered by myself, other students, laboratory assistant(s) and/or the course instructor. I acknowledge that the administration and performance of such tests are designed to be an educational experience.

Participation to medical tolerance is expected. If I feel I am medically unable or should not perform a given test, I will inform my lab instructor no later than the beginning of the lab session when that test is scheduled. If I have any condition which would make it unsafe for me to test another student, I will inform my lab instructor no later than the beginning of the lab session in which this is a possibility. I understand that practicing being an experimenter who can obtain good data is at least as much of the educational experience as is obtaining data on myself and evaluating/analyzing that.

There are certain risks associated with any physical testing. These include, but are not limited to, abnormal blood pressure or heart rate responses, heart beat disorders, fainting, and, in rare cases, heart attack, stroke or death. Muscle or joint injury, fatigue, as well as discomfort from wearing certain apparatus and having my finger pricked for small blood samples are also possible. Every effort will be made to minimize these risks by evaluation of preliminary information relating to my health status, by observation of symptoms during exercise tests and by guidance in properly performing the tests. This means that I will honestly and fully complete a medical history questionnaire during the first lab session, and that I will report any abnormal feelings of discomfort or pain associated with any lab session immediately to my lab instructor.

Throughout this laboratory experience, I will be required to share my test results with the lab staff and other class members which may include data being posted in or around the lab area. However, information about my laboratory results will not be disclosed for any other purposes without my written permission.

My enrollment in this course constitutes my consent to participate in these lab sessions within my health status and medical tolerance limits. If I have questions regarding any of the laboratory experiences, I am free to ask my lab or course instructor: (Name)____________________ (Phone Number)________________

______________________________ ____________________

Signature of Student Date

____

Signature of Witness

Please photocopy and retain a copy for yourself.

Reference

1. Modified from American College of Sports Medicine (1995). Guidelines for Exercise Testing and Prescription (5th ed.). Philadelphia, PA: Lea & Febiger.

Pre-Exercise Medical History[1,2]

Name: ______________________ Age: __________ Date: __________

Personal History

When was your last medical examination? __________

Have you ever had, or do you currently have any of the following conditions? Check (X) for any yes answers and circle the specific condition if more than one is given.

( ) 1. Heart attack, coronary angioplasty or cardiac surgery
( ) 2. Chest discomfort, especially with exercise
( ) 3. Lightheadedness or fainting with exercise
( ) 4. Exaggerated or excessive shortness of breath with exercise
( ) 5. Rapid heart beats or palpitations at rest
( ) 6. Heart murmur, clicks or other cardiac findings
( ) 7. High blood pressure
( ) 8. Stroke
( ) 9. Ankle swelling
( ) 10. Peripheral artery disease, claudication (calf pain or lameness while walking)
( ) 11. Phlebitis, emboli (inflammation or obstruction of blood vessel)
( ) 12. Pulmonary disease including asthma, emphysema and bronchitis
( ) 13. Abnormal blood lipids: cholesterol, triglycerides, VLDL, LDL or HDL
( ) 14. Diabetes.
( ) 15. Anemia
( ) 16. Emotional disorders
Specify: ______________________
( ) 17. Recent illness, hospitalization or surgical procedure
Specify: ______________________
( ) 18. Drug allergies
Specify: ______________________
( ) 19. Orthopedic problems, arthritis
Specify: ______________________
( ) 20. Pregnancy
Specify (if currently pregnant, indicate month): ______________________

Family History

Have any of your relatives (biological parents, grandparents, or siblings) had any of the following? Indicate who and age of occurrence.

( ) 1. Heart attack/sudden death
____

( ) 2. Heart operations (bypass, balloon angioplasty, pacemakers or valves)
____

( ) 3. High blood pressure
____

( ) 4. Lipid abnormalities (cholesterol, triglycerides, VLDL, LDL or HDL)
____

( ) 5. Diabetes
____

Personal Habits and Exercise History

1. List any medications you are currently taking and the condition for which each is prescribed.

____________________ ____________________

____________________ ____________________

2. Do you regularly ingest caffeine? ( ) Yes ( ) No
   Approximately how much per day? (Note: cola or coffee = 150 $\text{mg}\cdot 8\text{oz.}^{-1}$; tea = 100 $\text{mg}\cdot 8\text{ oz.}^{-1}$)______
3. Do you regularly ingest alcoholic beverages? ( ) Yes ( ) No
   Approximately how much per week? beer (8 oz. glass):______ wine (3 oz. glass):______
   hard liquor (1½ oz. drinks):______
4. Do you regularly smoke cigarettes? ( ) Yes ( ) No How many per day? ______
   If you do not currently smoke, have you ever smoked cigarettes? ( ) Yes ( ) No
   When did you stop smoking? __________
5. Present weight? ______ 1 year ago? ______ At age 21 yr.? ______ Height? ______
   Are you currently dieting to lose weight? ( ) Yes ( ) No
   Briefly describe your diet:____________________
   Have you ever been diagnosed for anorexia nervosa? ( ) Yes ( ) No
   Have you ever been diagnosed for bulemia? ( ) Yes ( ) No
6. Do you currently engage in an exercise training program? ( ) Yes ( ) No
   What is your exercise modality?____________________
   How many days per week do you exercise?____________________
   If you regularly check your heart rate while exercising, what is it?____________________
   Would you say your exercise sessions are: ( ) light, ( ) moderate, ( ) heavy or ( ) very heavy?
   How far do you walk each day? ____________________
   Is your occupation ( ) sedentary, ( ) lightly active, ( ) moderately active or ( ) very active?
   What is your occupation? ____________________

   Do you know of any reason why you should not engage in moderate to heavy exercise?( ) Yes ( ) No
   If yes, please specify: ____________________

References

1. American College of Sports Medicine (2000). Guidelines for Exercise Testing and Prescription (6th ed.) (pp. 35-36). Boston: Lea & Febiger.
2. Wilson, P.K. (1975). Adult Fitness and Cardiac Rehabilitation (p. 238). Baltimore: University Park Press.

Good Advice and Laboratory Goal

Read the introductory material in this lab manual: *Good Advice and Laboratory Goal*; *General But Important Information For Completing a Lab Write-Up*; *Know Your Verbs*; *Statistical Interpretations*; *Graphic Presentations*; *Footnotes and References*; and, *Answering an Exercise Physiology Question: An Example*. These pages contain important information that is crucial to properly completing your laboratory reports. Due to time constraints, the lab instructor may not be able to cover in class all of the procedures and guidelines outlined in the introductory section. Therefore, it is your responsibility to read the information presented, and, if you are uncertain about anything, to ask questions.

It is the aim of these laboratory experiences to not only provide you with data that will help you to understand and apply physiological concepts, but also to enhance your critical thinking and independent learning skills so that you may always be a learner and a thinker. To do this, you must become actively involved in the learning process, not just passively accept facts. To this end, it is important that you try to figure out the answers to your own questions before asking for help. On the other hand, it is important to ask for help if you still don't understand something after really trying to figure it out. No one can do the labs or learn the concepts for you, but with consistent attention to both process and outcomes of laboratory experiences, you can succeed.

This is a scientific course. You are the scientist; therefore, you must think, solve problems, ask questions, observe, deduce and learn.

General But Important Information For Completing a Lab Write-Up

Need to Know Information

1. Make sure you understand what the question is asking. Anytime you are asked to explain something physiologically, include not only *what* happens, but *how* it happens (i.e., what the mechanism of action is). On the following page is a list of verbs. Match each verb with its definition. Consult a dictionary if you are uncertain of any of the meanings. Use the precise meaning of each verb when answering the lab questions.

2. Double check all calculations. Prepare graphs according to the instructions given in the *Graphic Presentations* section. Look for general patterns in interpreting statistical results and graphs.

3. Present facts, data, analyses and discussions (citing references for any discussion), not opinions or unsubstantiated generalizations.

4. Answer all parts of the question very specifically. Always consult your textbook for expected physiological results; the *Related Readings* at the end of each lab may also provide additional information. Discuss key points and support them with the sources you have read. If you use a direct quote, follow it with an explanation in your own words to show your full understanding.

5. If a practical application is asked for, make sure that you give enough information that you could actually use it. Often you will not find these answers in a book but have to derive them from what you are learning.

6. Avoid inclusion of extraneous information; that is, do not ramble.

7. Be sure to *footnote and reference* all information and ideas which are not your own. This cannot be emphasized enough. Always credit the author when paraphrasing, and always use quotation marks when using a direct quote. Direct quotes should always be followed by an explanation in your own words: *You are not expected to make up scientific answers.*

8. If any question asks you to list examples, always list a minimum of two.

9. If asked to compare your data to norms, alway list your scores and the classification in which you fall (i.e., poor, good, average, etc.).

10. If you are ever unsure of what is expected of you, ask your lab or course instructor.

Know Your Verbs

These terms are action verbs frequently used in Exercise Physiology lab questions. Proper interpretation of these verbs will make doing the lab analysis, and probably quizzes and exams, easier.

Match the verb in Column I with its definition in Column II.

Column I	Column II
______ 1. Describe	a. explain or tell the meaning of
______ 2. Explain	b. examine so as to note the likeness of; point out similarities
______ 3. Distinguish	c. provide evidence of falsity by theoretical logic or scientific evidence; to argue against
______ 4. Define	d. support or justify by theoretical logic or scientific evidence; argue for
______ 5. Indicate	e. break down into relevant components and evaluate
______ 6. Determine	f. examine so as to note differences; point out dissimilarities
______ 7. Discuss	g. point out; show; express briefly; list and briefly describe
______ 8. Defend	h. recognize; identify points of difference
______ 9. Refute	i. decide conclusively; reach a decision after consideration or calculation
______ 10. Contrast	j. give an account of in words; provide details of what occurred
______ 11. Compare	k. make understandable; clarify based on scientific mechanisms (underlying physiology) or theory
______ 12. Interpret	l. consider or examine through discourse; present everything important about this issue
______ 13. Analyze	m. state the specific meaning of without using the word itself; not equivalent with calculation of

Statistical Interpretations[1]

Note to Student: In this Exercise Physiology class, the goal is not that you learn how to calculate or run statistical tests, but that you are able to use statistical information to interpret physiological or fitness experimental results.

Central Tendency and Dispersion

1. **Mean (M)**: The mean of a numerical data set is the arithmetic average; it is calculated by summing all the numbers within a data set and dividing by the number of data points. For example, given the data set, 5 m, 10 m, 13 m, 14 m, 7 m, 8 m, 9 m, the mean would be calculated as follows:

$$(5\text{ m} + 10\text{ m} + 13\text{ m} + 14\text{ m} + 7\text{ m} + 8\text{ m} + 9\text{ m}) \div 7 = 66 \div 7 = 9.43\text{ m}$$

   What is the mean of the data set, 123 cm, 134 cm, 132 cm, 145 cm, 112 cm, 116 cm and 165 cm?

2. **Standard Deviation (SD)**: The standard deviation is a measure of spread within the data set; variation refers to how far the numbers within the data set fall from the mean. For example, consider the following data set from the earlier example: 5 m, 10 m, 13 m, 14 m, 7 m, 8 m, 9m. The mean of this data set is 9.43 m, and the standard deviation is 2.96 m. Therefore, if a data point is within one standard deviation of the mean, it is between 6.47 m and 12.39 m; that is, 9.43 m - 2.96 m and 9.43 m + 2.96 m.

   What would the range be for a data point that fell within 2 standard deviations of the mean?

Degree of Relationship

1. **Pearson Product Moment Correlation (r):** A correlation coefficient is a number ranging from -1.00 to +1.00 which indicates the degree of the relationship between two variables (e.g., the relationship between percent body fat and the 1 mile run time). The number denotes the strength of the relationship between two variables, and the sign (-, +) indicates the direction of the relationship. A positive (+, direct) correlation coefficient indicates that as one variable increases, the other variable increases; a negative (-, inverse) correlation coefficient indicates that as one variable increases, the other variable decreases. It is important to note, however, that a strong relationship between two variables does not necessarily mean that the relationship is cause and effect.

   Rule of thumb for interpreting the strength of a correlation:
   - 0.00 - 0.29: low relationship
   - 0.30 - 0.59: moderate relationship
   - 0.60 - 0.84: moderately high relationship
   - 0.85 - 1.00: high relationship

   Do not let the sign (+ or -) confuse you. An r of -1.00 has the same strength as a +1.00, an r of -0.30 has the same strength as a +0.30 and an r of -0.0001 has the same strength as an r of +0.0001. The only thing that is different is the direction of the relationship denoted by the sign that preceeds the number (see page 14 for examples of positive and negative correlations). The following paragraph is an example of how the correlation coefficient may be used.

In order to determine the validity of the PACER test in estimating maximal oxygen consumption (VO_2 max), 100 students performed an incremental work test to maximum on the treadmill to determine their VO_2 max using indirect spirometry. One week later, the same students performed the PACER field test in order to estimate their VO_2 max. A Pearson Correlation was calculated to determine the relationship between the students' scores on the PACER field test and their VO_2 max values measured during the treadmill test. The hypothetical data are presented below:

N (the number of people in the study): 100
r (correlation coefficient): 0.84
p (probability): 0.0002

How would you describe the relationship between the results of the PACER field test and the results from the incremental work test to maximum on the treadmill? Is the PACER a valid field test for estimating VO_2 max ?

Types of Significance

1. **Statistical** significance relies on the laws of probability to determine whether an observed difference between means is too large or too small to occur by chance. Probability is denoted by a p-value. Generally, the p-value must be less than 0.05 to be statistically significant. This means that the probability is less than 5 times out of 100 that the results occurred by chance (0.05 x 100 = 5). Although a standard may be set for statistical significance, it is important to note that there is no actual cut-off for statistical significance, only increasing levels of significance. Therefore, if you wanted to be extremely confident that your results were not due to chance, you can set your standard higher:

   $p< 0.01$ — probability is less than 1 out of 100
   $p< 0.002$ — probability is less than 2 out of 1000
   $p< 0.0003$ — probability is less than 3 out of 10,000

   Try not to be confused with numbers presented as decimals: 0.01 is less than 0.05, 0.002 is less than 0.05, 0.0003 is less than 0.05 and 0.00004 is less than 0.05; however, 0.06 is greater than 0.05, 0.1 is greater than 0.05 and 0.2 is greater than 0.05.

2. **Practical** significance relies on shared variance to determine how much of an effect one variable has on another variable, or the amount of variability in one variable that is explained by the other variable. To determine practical significance, you must calculate a coefficient of determination; this is calculated by squaring the r value and multiplying by 100 (r^2 x 100). For example, if the correlation coefficient between percent body fat and 1 mile run time were 0.78 for a group of 100 individuals, the coefficient of determination would be 61%. This means that 61% of the variability in 1 mile run times is due to the individuals having different percentages of body fat. Generally, the shared variance must be greater than 50% to have practical significance. Look back to the VO_2 max data. Did the results occur by chance? What is the shared variance? Do the results have practical significance? Go to page 14 and determine the practical significance for each of the three relationships shown.

Tests for Determining Statistical Significance

1. <u>t-test</u>: The t-test is used to determine if there is a significant difference between two means. For example, to determine if athletic individuals have a lower resting heart rate than sedentary people, the

following experiment could be performed: Select 20 athletes and 20 sedentary individuals and measure their resting heart rates. Sum the heart rates from each group and divide by 20 to get the mean scores for the athletes and sedentary individuals. Run a t-test. If the p-value is less than 0.05, then there is a significant difference between the resting heart rates of athletes and sedentary individuals. The hypothetical data may be presented as follows:

Resting Heart Rates of Athletes and Sedentary Individuals (N=40)		
	Athlete	Sedentary
Mean	46 b·min^{-1}	72 b·min^{-1}
Standard Deviation	4 b·min^{-1}	7 b·min^{-1}
Difference Between Means	26 b·min^{-1}	
t-score Probability	2.37 p <0.0001	

Is the difference between the means statistically significant? How can you tell?

2. **Analysis of Variance (ANOVA)**: ANOVA is used to determine if there is a significant difference between three or more means. For example, if you wanted to compare the lactate response between four different exercises, the following experiment could be performed: Randomly select 30 people and have them perform a 20 minute bike ride at a heart rate of 135 b·min^{-1}, a 10 second Wingate Speed Test (WST), a 30 second Wingate Anaerobic Test (WAT) and 4 sets of 15 RM on the bench press with 1 minute rest between each set on four separate days. Measure the blood lactate before and after each bout of exercise, and determine the change in blood lactate for each individual after each test. Sum the lactate responses for each group and divide by 30 to get the mean score for each test. Run an ANOVA; if $p< 0.05$, then there is a significant difference between the lactate responses to the four different types of exercise. Although the ANOVA determines statistical significance, it does not tell you where the significant difference lies — is it between all four exercises, or just the 20 minute bike ride and the 30 second WAT? To determine where the significant difference lies, a *follow-up* test would have to be run to determine how large a difference is needed between any two means in order to be statistically significant. The hypothetical results may be presented as follows:

Lactate Response to 4 Different Exercises (N=30)			
	Mean	Standard Deviation	Probability
20 Minute Bike Ride	2.1 mmol·L^{-1}	0.6 mmol·L^{-1}	$p< 0.05$
10 s WST	1.8 mmol·L^{-1}	0.3 mmol·L^{-1}	
30 s WAT	10.8 mmol·L^{-1}	2.6 mmol·L^{-1}	
4 x 15 RM	6.7 mmol·L^{-1}	1.3 mmol·L^{-1}	
Minimum difference needed for significance: 2.0 mmol·L^{-1}			

Knowing the minimum difference, determine which conditions are significantly different from each other.

Reference

1. Baumgartner, T.A. & Jackson (1999). Measurement for Evaluation in Physical Education and Exercise (6th ed.). Boston: WCB\McGraw-Hill.

Graphic Presentations

Graphs are pictoral presentations used to present data and reveal patterns that exist in data. They act as visual summaries of data. Three types of graphs will be used in presenting data obtained in labs: Line graphs, bar graphs and scattergrams. The following are some helpful guidelines for preparing graphs.

Note to Student: If your graphs are not computer generated, your instructor may specify a specific size graph paper (e.g., 10 mm·cm^{-1} or 20 squares·inch^{-1}). Be sure to determine this prior to preparing your graphs.

Line Graphs

1. Must have a title.
2. Each axis must have a label which includes appropriate units of measure (e.g., blood pressure — mmHg).
3. Each division along the axis must be equal in length, designating equal amounts of units.
4. The vertical axis (Y or ordinate) should be approximately 2/3 to 3/4 the length of the horizontal axis (X or abscissa).
5. Lines connecting data points should be drawn in a straight line from one point to the next: Use a ruler.
6. A key must be provided when using different symbols on the graph.
7. Units can be condensed on the vertical axis prior to plotting data; that is, the axis does not have to start at 0. The independent variable, the variable manipulated, is put on the X axis. The dependent variable, the variable that you are curious about, is put on the Y axis. For example, if you want to know how changing the intensity of exercise effects VO_2, intensity would be the independent variable and VO_2 would be the dependent variable.
8. Time and/or workrate, if used, should be on the X axis.

Bar Graphs

1. Must have a title.
2. The vertical axis must have a label which includes units.
3. Each division along the vertical axis must be equal in length.
4. Bars must be labeled along the horizontal axis.
5. Bars should be of equal width and spaced evenly.
6. A key must be provided when using different symbols on the graph.
7. The vertical axis must start at zero and cannot be condensed.

Scattergrams

1. Must have a title.
2. Each axis must have a label which includes appropriate units of measure (e.g., blood pressure — mmHg).
3. Each division along the axis must be equal in length, designating equal amounts of units.
4. The vertical axis (Y or ordinate) should be approximately 2/3 to 3/4 the length of the horizontal axis (X or abscissa).
5. A line of best fit is drawn with a ruler. The line of best fit is a line that separates the data points into two even halves in the direction of the data points.
6. A key must be provided when using different symbols on the graph.
7. Units can be condensed on the vertical axis prior to plotting data; that is, the axis does not have to start at 0.
8. Time and/or workrate, if used, should be on the X axis.

Sample of Line Graphs

Heart Rate Response to Short-Term Aerobic Exercise

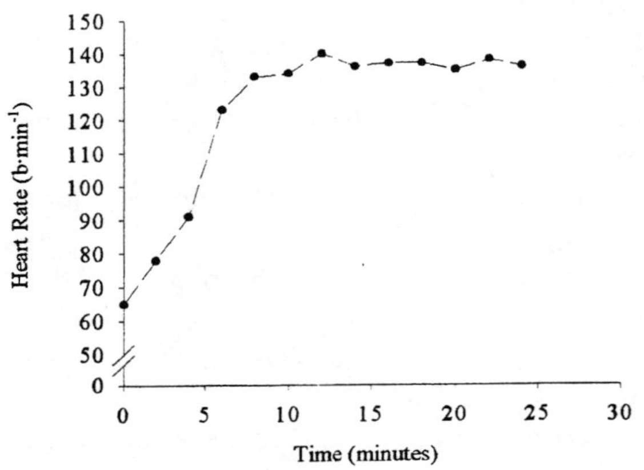

Heart Rate Response to Incremental Cycle Ergometry

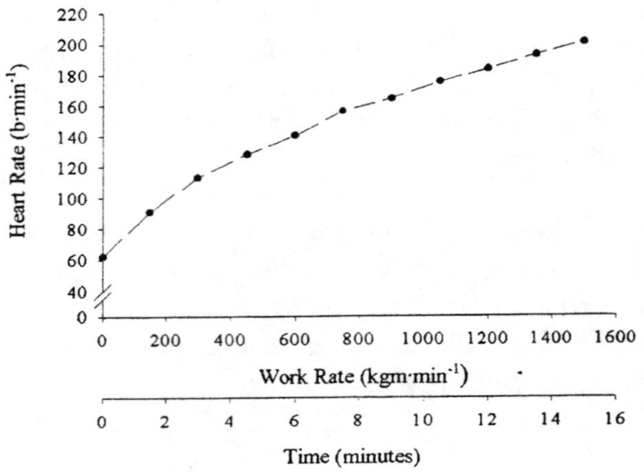

Heart Rate Response to Prolonged Aerobic Exercise

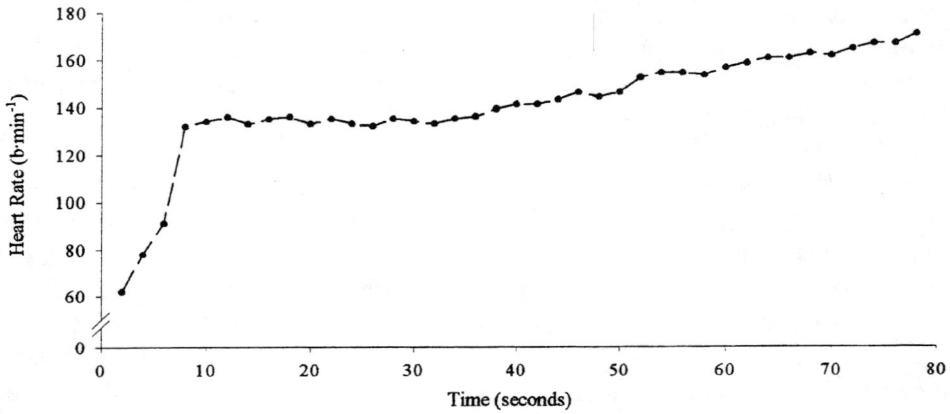

Heart Rate Response to 2 Minute Static Contraction

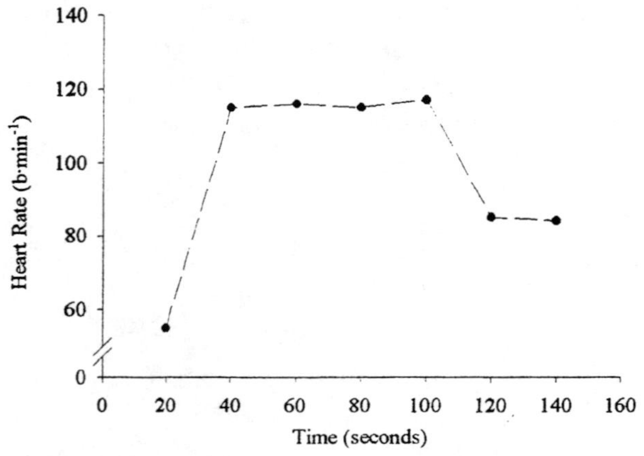

Heart Rate Response to Leg Press Exercise

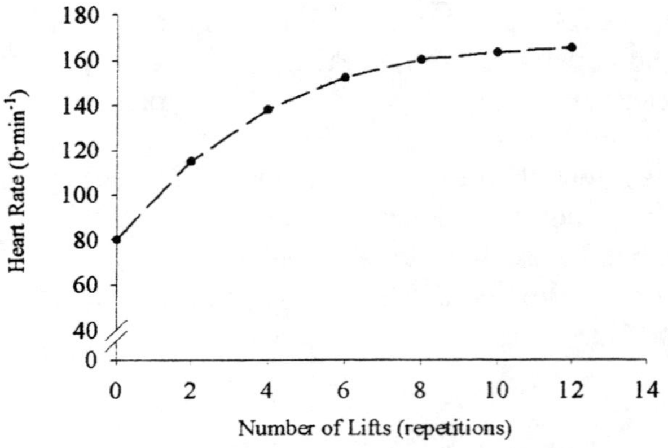

Sample of a Bar Graph

Blood Pressure Adaptations in Response to Exercise Training and Medication

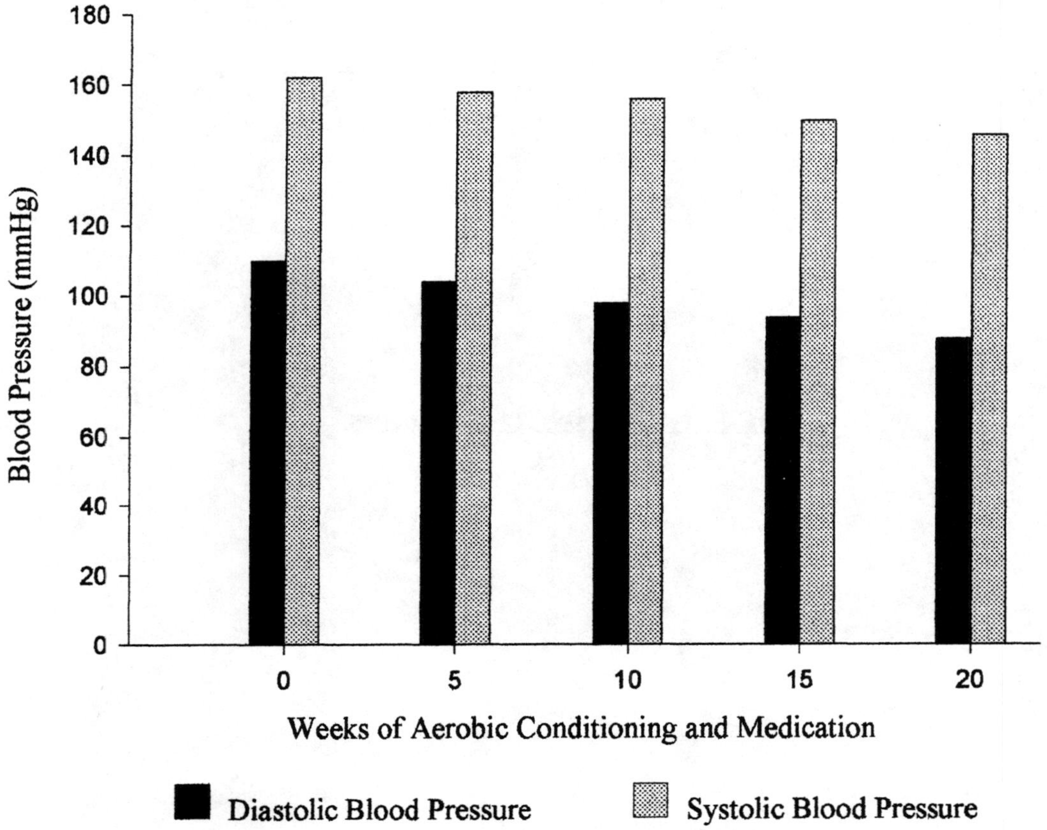

Sample of Scattergrams

Height vs. Age

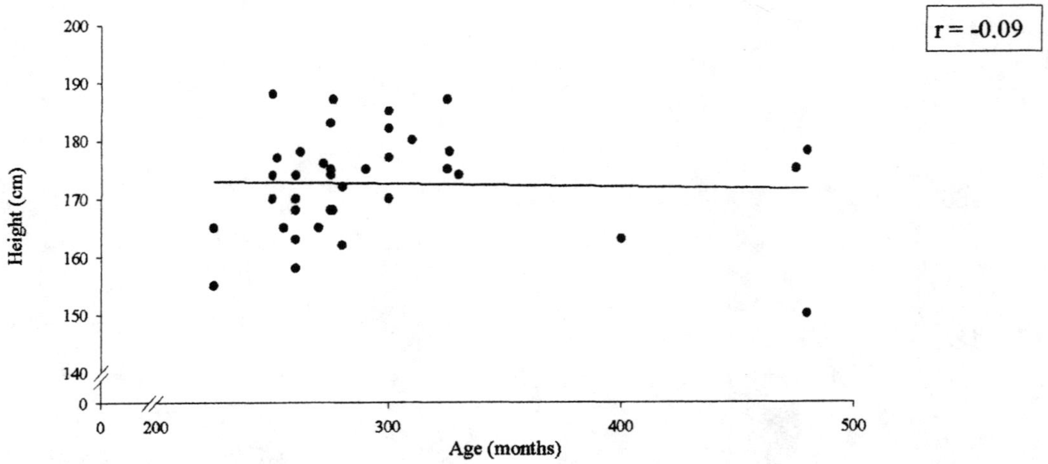

PACER Levels vs. Oxygen Consumption

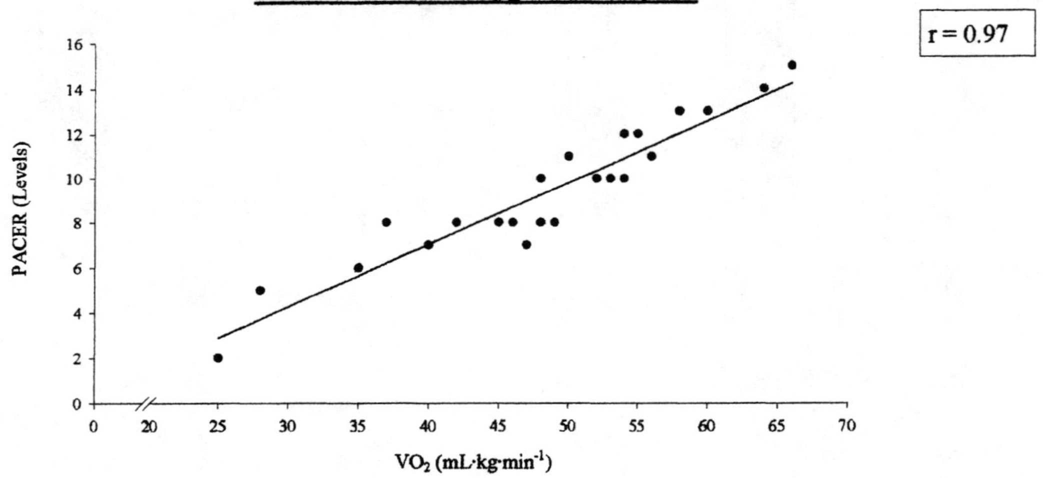

Body Fat vs. Body Density

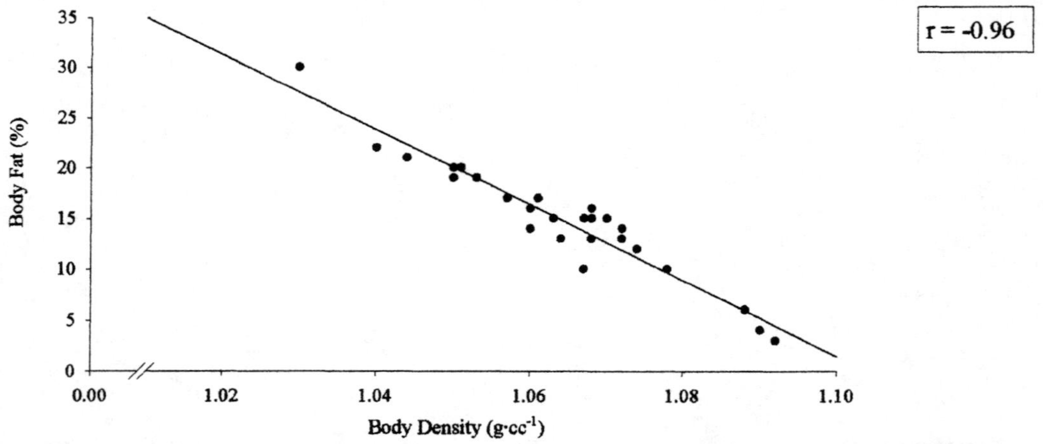

Footnotes and References

Footnoting

A. Direct Quote

The cited direct text is put in quotation marks:

"...the capacity of the heart muscle to increase the cardiac output is greater than the ability of the muscle to receive it..." (Consolazio et al., 1963, p. 357).

B. Paraphrasing

Any idea that is not your own must be referenced (i.e., you read and used information out of a book or periodical but did not quote it directly). An example follows:

There is a high correlation between VO_2 max and maximum heart rate, so it has been assumed, since heart rate cannot be increased with age, it is a limiting factor in VO_2 max (Simpson, 1990).

As shown above, for a direct quote, the page number must be included in the footnote; for information from a book that is paraphrased, however, the page numbers should be included in the full reference.

There are several formats that may be used for proper footnoting and referencing. Your instructor may wish you to use a particular format. Make sure you know which format you are supposed to use. The following examples show the important elements of a footnote or reference that should be included no matter what format is being used. The format used here is according to the American Psychological Association (1994).[1]

Reference Examples

You should list the authors of works cited in alphabetical order. This should be the last page of your lab write-up.

A. Book

Consolazio, C.F., Johnson, R. E. & Pecora, L. J. (1963). Physiological Measurements of Metabolic Functions in Man. New York: McGraw-Hill.

B. Book Chapter

Gettman, L.R. (1989). Fitness Testing. In American College of Sports Medicine (Eds.). Resource Manual for Guidelines for Exercise Testing and Prescription (pp.161-170). Philidelphia: Lea & Febiger.

C. Journal

Klissouras, V. (1971). "Heritability of adaptive variation." Journal of Applied Physiology, 31 (3), 338-334.

D. Internet

Merriman, B. (1996). Periodized Weight- lifting Routines [on-line]. Available: http://segment. UCSF. edu/ brent/ fitness/ barry.htm

Other Format Manuals

1. CBE Style Manual Committee (1995). Scientific Style and Format: The CBE Manual for Authors, Editors and Publishers (6th ed.). New York: Cambridge University Press.
2. Rubens, P. (2001). Science and Technical Writing: A Manual of Style. New York: Routledge.

Reference

1. American Psychological Association (2001). Publication Manual of the American Psychological Association (5th ed.). Washigton, D.C.: American Psychological Association.

Answering an Exercise Physiology Question: An Example

The example question is: *Explain what RPP means physiologically. How may it be used in a practical situation?* (3 points)

1. Student 1's Response: RPP means rate pressure product.

   Student 1's grade: 0 points.

   Why? Only what RPP stands for was stated. Student 1 did not answer the question. No credit is given.

2. Student 2's Response: RPP is the rate pressure product when measured by heart rate multiplied by blood pressure divided by 100.

   Student 2's grade: 0 points.

   Why? This information is given on the lab sheet; thus, it is redundant and only describes the calculation procedure. No credit is given.

3. Student 3's Response: RPP is the abbreviation for rate pressure product. It is an estimate of myocardial oxygen consumption.

   Student 3's grade: approximately 1 point.

   Why? This individual did not reference this paraphrased information, nor did he/she explain the practicality of RPP.

4. Student 4's Response: RPP is the rate pressure product which is determined by [HR x BP] ÷ 100. This can be calculated while at rest or during exercise (Plowman & Smith, 2003). According to Lamb (1986, p. 19), RPP is "An index of myocardial oxygen consumption." This provides the physiologist with an estimate of the amount of work done by the heart. This differs from the total work of the whole body which would be indicated if heart rate alone was monitored (Katch, 1987). This measure is important to the physiologists when working with cardiac rehab patients. The physiologist can better understand an individual's response to exercise when measuring RPP, and it adds to the safety of the exercise program.

   Student 4's grade: 2 points.

   Why? This individual stated what RPP stood for and what it measured. He/she also referenced all information (i.e., paraphrased and used direct quotes). It was also stated why RPP is important to the exercise physiologist, and a practical example of its use was given. This individual did not receive full credit, however, because he/she was too nonspecific in terms of the interpretation of the example.

   Student 5's Response: RPP is the rate pressure product which is determined by [HR x BP] ÷ 100. This can be calculated while at rest or during exercise (Plowman & Smith, 1997). According to Lamb (1986, p. 19), RPP is "An index of myocardial oxygen consumption." This provides the physiologist with an estimate of the amount of work done by the heart. This differs from the total work of the whole body which would be indicated if heart rate alone was monitored (Katch, 1987). This measure is important to the physiologists when working with cardiac rehab patients. The physiologist can better understand the individual's response to exercise when measuring RPP, and it adds to the safety of the exercise program. If the increase in RPP is too large for a low workrate, it may indicate the body's inability to regulate pressure, thereby causing strain on the vessels and heart (Brooks, 1987). Low or no increase in RPP may be due to poor chronotropic (heart rate) response to exercise, an inability of the heart to increase cardiac output and/or a large decrease in total peripheral resistance (DeVries, 1985). In either case, further evaluation is warranted, and the RPP levels need to be considered in prescribing the exercise (Plowman, 1990). One should limit exercise intensity to normal response loads if these are different from threshold heart rate values (Wilmore, 1987).

Student 5's grade: 3 points.

5. Why? The student very thoroughly covered all facets of the question and footnoted the appropriate information. A reference list, not reproduced here, was also included.

Work, Power and Conversions

Graphic Presentations and Statistical Interpretations

Student Learning Objectives

After completing this lab, you should be able to:

1. Define, explain and correctly use key terms.
2. List the fundamental measures, derived measures and the units of measurement for each.
3. Calculate force, work and power.
4. Convert units from English to metric.
5. Convert oxygen consumption from $L \cdot min^{-1}$ to $mL \cdot kg^{-1} \cdot min^{-1}$ and vice versa.
6. Interpret correlation coefficients and the results of t-tests and analyses of variance (ANOVAs).

Equipment

- Scale
- Stadiometer

Procedure: Part I

All students should familiarize themselves with the following fundamental measures, derived measures, units of measurement and conversions before proceeding to the calculation and experimental portion of the lab.

A. Fundamental Measures: The International Metric System - Le Systeme International d' Unites (SI)

There are 5 basic metric units used in Exercise Physiology			
SI Unit	**Measure**	**Abbreviation**	**English Unit**
meter *liter	length *volume	m *L or l	inches fluid ounces
kilogram	mass	kg	pounds
°celsius	temperature	°C	farenheit
second	time	s	second
mole	amount of substance	mol	
* The liter is a derivative of the meter ($0.001\ m^3 = 1\ L$).			

B. Derived Measures: Force, Work, Power and Density

Derived measures are those that are derived from the fundamental measures.

1. Force
   = mass (kg) x accleration ($m \cdot s^{-2}$)
   = mass (kg) x velocity ($m \cdot s^{-1}$)/time (s)
   = mass x [(distance/time)/time]

2. Work
   = force (N) x distance (m)
   = [mass x (distance/time)/time] x distance
   = mass x acceleration x distance

3. Power
   = work (J)/time (s)
   = [mass x (distance/time)/time) x distance]/time
   = work/time
   = force x velocity

4. Density
   = mass (kg)/volume (L)

C. Units of Measurement

1. Force
   = kg x ($m \cdot s^{-1}$)s^{-1}
   = kg x ($m \cdot s^{-2}$)
   = 1 Newton (N)

A Newton is a force that gives a mass of 1 kg an acceleration of 1 m·s^{-2}. An old unit of force is the kilopond (kp). One kp is a force acting on a mass of 1 kg at normal acceleration due to gravity: 1 kp = 9.80655 N.

2. Work
   = Newton (N) x meter (m)
   = Joule (J)

Work is done when a force acts against a resistance to produce motion. It is the product of the force and the distance moved. One joule of work is done when the force of 1 N moves through a distance of 1 m. Because the effect of gravity on 1 kg is nearly constant at all places on earth, work is expressed in kg·m: 1 kgm = 9.80655 J.

3. Power
   = (N x m)s^{-1}
   = J·s^{-1}
   = 1 Watt

Power is the rate of doing work. It is expressed in kgm·min^{-1}: 1 kgm·min^{-1} = 0.1635 W.

4. Density
   = mass (kg)/volume (m^3)

Density is the amount of mass per unit volume. In the metric system, water has a density of 1 gram per cubic centimeter (g·cc^{-1}) or 1000 kg per cubic meter (1000 kg·m^3).

D. Conversion Factors

1. Length

1 inch = 2.54 cm	1 cm = 0.394 in
1 foot = 30.48 cm	1 mile = 1610 m
1 meter = 39.37 in	1 km = 0.62 mile
1 meter = 3.28 ft	1 yard = 0.914 m

2. Volume

1 quart = 0.94 L	1 mL = 1 cc
1 L = 1.06 quarts	1 fl. oz. = 29.5 mL

3. Mass
   1 kg = 2.2 lbs. = 9.80655 Newtons*
   1 lb. = 0.454 kg

* When gravity equals 9.8 m·s^{-2}. 9.8 m·s^{-2} is the acceleration of an object due to the force of gravity.

4. Force
   1 lb. = 4.45 N
   1 N = 0.225 lbs.
   1 kg = 1 kp*

* Under normal acceleration of gravity.

5. Power
   1 horsepower (hp) = 746 W
   1 W = 6.12 kp·m·min^{-1}

E. Metric Prefixes

Prefixes particularly relevant to exercise physiology are given below:

Prefix	Value	Symbol
Mega	1,000,000 (10^6)	M
Kilo	1,000 (10^3)	k
Hecto	100 (10^2)	h
Deca	10	da
Deci	0.1 (10^{-1})	d
Centi	0.01 (10^{-2})	c
Milli	0.001 (10^{-3})	m
Micro	0.000001 (10^{-6})	µ

The metric system is based on 10, just like the United States' monetary system.

10 mm = 1 cm	10 m = 1 dam
10 cm = 1dm	10 dam = 1 hm
10 dm = 1m	10 hm = 1 km

F. Metric Math

1. When you are working from the base unit to

smaller units, move the decimal point to the right.

2. When you are working from the base unit to larger units, move the decimal point to the left.

1000 meters	1 kilometer	1 km
100 meters	1 hectometer	1 hm
10 meters	1 dekameter	1 dam
Base unit	**1 meter**	**1 m**
0.1 meter	1 decimeter	1 dm
0.01 meter	1 centimeter	1 cm
0.001 meter	1 millimeter	1 mm

Examples:

19.6 m = 196 dm = 1960 cm = 19, 600 mm
19.6 m = 1.96 dam = 0.0196 hm = 0.0196 km
1 L = 10 dL = 100 cL = 1000 mL

3. Within the metric system, as in the English system, values can be expressed in absolute or relative units.

Examples:

a) Assuming a body weight of 50 kg:

$$2.1 \text{ L·min}^{-1} = \frac{2100 \text{ mL·min}^{-1}}{50 \text{ kg}}$$

$$= 42.0 \text{ mL·kg}^{-1}\text{·min}^{-1}$$

b) Assuming a body weight of 60 kg:

$$35 \text{ mL·kg}^{-1}\text{·min}^{-1} \text{ x } 60 \text{ Kg} = \frac{2100 \text{ mL·min}^{-1}}{1000 \text{ mL·L}^{-1}}$$

$$= 2.10 \text{ L·min}^{-1}$$

G. Converting Units

To convert from one set of units to another, set up an *equation of equivalencies* which will allow you to cancel unwanted units and leave the desired units.

Examples:

1. Convert 80 km·hr^{-1} to m·s^{-1}. Equivalencies needed: 1000 m per 1 km; 1 hour per 60 minutes; 1 minute per 60 seconds.

$$\frac{1 \text{ hr}}{60 \text{ min}} \text{ x } \frac{1 \text{ min}}{60 \text{ s}} = \frac{1 \text{ hr}}{3600 \text{ s}}$$

$$\frac{80 \text{ km}}{1 \text{ hr}} \text{ x } \frac{1000 \text{ m}}{1 \text{ km}} \text{ x } \frac{1 \text{ hr}}{3600 \text{ s}}$$

$$\frac{80,000 \text{ m}}{3600 \text{ s}} = 22.2 \text{ m·s}^{-1}$$

2. Convert 160 lbs. to kg. Equivalencies needed: 1 kg per 2.2 pounds.

$$160 \text{ lbs. x } \frac{1\text{kg}}{2.2 \text{ lbs.}}$$

$$\frac{160 \text{ kg}}{2.2} = 72.2 \text{ kg}$$

3. Convert 6 feet and 4 inches into meters. Equivalencies needed: 1 m per 39.37 in.

6’ x 12” + 4 = 76 in.

$$76 \text{ in. x } \frac{1 \text{ m}}{39.37 \text{ in.}} = 1.93 \text{ m}$$

4. Convert 10,000 m to miles. Equivalencies needed: 1 mile per 1610 meters.

$$10,000 \text{ m x } \frac{1 \text{ mile}}{1610 \text{ m}} = 6.21 \text{ miles}$$

5. If a person lifted 325 lbs. off the floor, how much force was exerted? Equivalencies needed: 1 N per 0.225lbs.

$$325 \text{ lbs. x } \frac{1 \text{ N}}{0.225 \text{ lbs.}} = 1444.4 \text{ N}$$

Procedure: Part II

Height, weight and age will be obtained from all students, and the data will be used to create scattergrams. Students should work with a partner and measure each other's height and weight.

Protocols

A. Height Measurement

1. Remove your shoes.
2. If a stadiometer is used, face away from the wall. If a scale is used, face away from the vertical rod.
3. Stand against the wall with your heels together, and evenly distribute your weight over each foot. Keep your chin level, eyes looking straight ahead and place your hands on hips.
4. Inhale deeply: Your partner takes the measurement at the highest point on the head while gently, but firmly, compressing the hair. The measurement is taken to the nearest 0.1 cm or 0.25 in.

> *Note: After measuring the height, check to make sure the scale was read correctly.*

5. Record the height in Data Table 1.0.

B. Weight Measurement: Control Condition

> *Note: Normal laboratory measurement of weight should always be done without shoes and wearing as little clothing as possible (preferably shorts and a t-shirt).*

1. Remove your shoes and step on the center of the scale.
2. Face toward the beam of the scale and evenly distribute your weight over each foot.
3. Your partner stands on the other side of the scale and moves the beam weights until balance is achieved. Weight is recorded to the nearest 0.25 lb. or 0.01 kg.

> *Note: After measuring the weight, check to make sure the scale was read correctly.*

4. Return the beam weights to zero.
5. Record the weight in Data Table 1.0.

C. Weight Measurement: Experimental Condition

1. Step on the center of the scale with your shoes on.
2. Repeat steps 2-5 from Protocol B.

D. Age Conversion

1. Calculate your age in months.
2. Record the age in Data Table 1.0.

Data Table 1.0				
Subject	Height (cm) Without Shoes	Weight (kg) Without shoes	Weight (kg) With Shoes	Age (months)
1				
2				
3				
4				
5				
6				
7				
8				
9				
10				
11				
12				
13				
14				
15				
16				
17				
18				
19				
20				
Mean				
SD				

Student Activities

A. Definitions.

Define the following key terms. For those terms which are measurable variables, describe in your own words what they mean (not how they are obtained or calculated). Indicate the unit(s) of measurement.

1. Density:

2. Force:

3. Mass:

4. Power:

5. Units of Measurement:

6. Velocity:

7. Work:

B. Analysis.

1. Using the class data in Data Table 1.0, graph the following as scattergrams and briefly discuss the relationship between the variables.
   a. Height vs. Weight Without Shoes
   b. Age vs. Weight Without Shoes
   c. Weight With Shoes vs. Weight Without Shoes
   d. Age vs. Height

C. Interpretation and Analysis.

1. Complete the following practice graph scenarios. First, choose which type of graph would be the best graph to depict the data. Then, based on the graph you complete, briefly discuss the relationship between the variables.

   a. To determine her acute blood pressure response to incremental aerobic exercise, Julie rode the cycle ergometer for 18 minutes. She started at a light workrate, and she increased the workrate every three minutes. The results of her exercise bout are presented in Table A. Graphically show the acute systolic blood pressure (SBP) and diastolic blood pressure (DBP) response to incremental aerobic exercise and briefly discuss the relationship between the variables.

Table A

Time (minutes)	Workrate ($kgm \cdot min^{-1}$)	SBP (mmHg)	DBP (mmHg)
Rest	0	114	64
3	150	126	68
6	300	136	64
9	450	138	64
12	600	146	66
15	750	156	66
18	900	168	64

   b. At the same time Julie started an aerobic exercise program, Tim started a strength training program. An exercise physiologist measured the capillary density of Tim and Julie's vastus lateralis before they started their respective training programs and after 6 months of training. Given the results in Table B, graphically show how capillary density changes in response to aerobic training and strength training and briefly discuss the relationship between the variables.

Table B

	Capillary Density ($capillaries \cdot mm^{-2}$)	
	Pre-Training	Post-Training
Julie	307	362
Tim	332	315

D. Application.

Complete the following problems. Show all of your calculation set-ups.

1. A person weighing 135 lbs. steps up and down on a bench for 5 minutes at a rate of 30 $steps \cdot min^{-1}$. The bench is 20 cm high. Calculate work and power for the first 30 seconds.

2. One person doing a bench press raises 150 lbs. 0.5 meters 10 times, while another person raises 130 lbs. 0.4 meters 15 times. Which person has done more work?

3. A woman holds an 8 lb. shot put 0.34 meters above the floor for 10 seconds. How much work is done holding the shot put?

4. According to a simplified model of the human heart, with each pulse approximately 20 g of blood is accelerated from 0.25 $m \cdot s^{-1}$ to 0.35 $m \cdot s^{-1}$ during a period of 0.10 seconds. Given that the 20 g of blood is moved about 0.30 m for each beat, and the heart beats about 60 $beats \cdot min^{-1}$, how much work is done by the heart in one day? Hint: Acceleration is the difference between final velocity and initial velocity divided by time.

5. A 70 kg hiker climbs to the top of a 4,200 m mountain. The climb is made in 4.0 hours starting at an elevation of 3,100 m. Calculate work and power output.

6. A person pedals a cycle ergometer as fast as possible for 30 seconds against a resistance of 4 kg. If the total number of pedal revolutions completed in 30 seconds is 52.5, calculate work and power (Note: On this bike, for each revolution a point on the wheel travels 6 m). Hint: When pedaling a cycle ergometer, the resistance is due to a weight which must be lifted against the force of gravity.

7. A person who weighs 163 lbs. runs up a stairway 1.02 m high in 1.203 seconds. Calculate work and power. Hint: Whenever an object (e.g., your body) is lifted against the force of gravity, acceleration is the acceleration due to gravity.

Related Readings

1. Plowman, S.A. & Smith, D.L. (2003). Exercise Physiology for Health, Fitness and Performance (2nd ed.). San Fransisco: Benjamin Cummings.
2. Powers, S.K. & Howley, E.T. (2001). Exercise Physiology: Theory and Application to Fitness and Performance (4th ed.) (pp. 98-103). Boston: McGraw-Hill.
3. McArdle, W.D., Katch, F.I. & Katch, V.L. (2001). Exercise Physiology: Energy, Nutrition and Human Performance (5th ed.) (pp. 1051-162). Baltimore: Williams & Wilkins.

Responses to Different Categories of Exercise

Integration and Analysis

Student Learning Objectives

After completing this lab, you should be able to:

1. Define, explain and correctly use key terms.
2. Describe how to collect data on the exercise response to five categories of exercise.
3. Analyze the respiratory responses to different categories of exercise.
4. Analyze cardiovascular responses to different catagories of exercise.
5. Analyze the metabolic responses to different catagories of exercise.

Equipment

- Barbell and Weight Plates (5-75 lbs./2-35 kg)
- Handgrip or Other Dynamometer (optional)
- Heart Rate Watches/Transmitter Straps
- Lactate Analyzer and Accessories
- Motordriven Treadmill or Cycle Ergometer
- O_2 and CO_2 Analyzers
- Pneumoscan Flow Meter or Pneumotach
- Sphygmomanometer/Cuff/Stethoscope

Procedure

The respiratory, cardiovascular and metabolic responses to the following 5 categories of exercise will be examined: short-term, light to moderate submaximal aerobic exercise, long-term, moderate to heavy submaximal aerobic exercise, incremental exercise to maximum, static exercise and dynamic resistance exercise. Determine which students will be subjects. Suggestions:

- The same student or all students perform all five protocols.
- A different student performs each of the five protocols.
- One male and one female of equal training status perform all five protocols.
- Two or three students of the same sex but different training status perform all five protocols.

During each activity, the following variables will be measured:

- Blood Pressure (BP)
- Frequency of Breathing (f)
- Heart Rate (HR)
- Lactate ($[La^-]$)
- Oxygen Consumption (VO_2)
- Rate of Perceived Exertion (RPE)
- Respiratory Exchange Ratio (RER)
- Tidal Volume (V_T)

These variables are measured and recorded as indicated on the respective exercise data sheet or by the instructor (more or fewer samples may be taken).

<u>Note to Instructor</u>: Any or all exercise categories can be selected for data collection and subsequent analysis. Likewise, any or all of the variables may be included in the data collection and subsequent analysis. If individuals of varying training status are used as subjects, or if pre-post training data are collected, training adaptations can also be analyzed.

Protocols

Note to Student: The lab instructor will inform you of the desired time span for recovery data collection.

A. Short-Term, Light to Moderate Submaximal Aerobic Exercise

1. Sit quietly for 3 minutes. When gas analysis data indicates relaxation and a true resting state, 3 minutes of resting data are obtained. Gas analysis is continuous from that point.
2. Walk on the treadmill at 3.5 $mi\cdot hr^{-1}$ at 0% grade for 10 minutes or cycle at 50 $rev\cdot min^{-1}$ at 1 kp or 1.5 kp (50-75 watts) for 10 minutes.
3. Sit quietly for 5-15 minutes of recovery.

B. Long-Term, Moderate to Heavy Submaximal Aerobic Exercise

1. Sit quietly for 3 minutes. When gas analysis data indicates relaxation and a true resting state, 3 minutes of resting data are obtained. Gas analysis is continuous from that point.
2. Run on a treadmill at a self-selected constant speed (5, 6 or 7 $mi\cdot hr^{-1}$) or cycle at 50 $rev\cdot min^{-1}$ at 2.5, 3 or 3.5 kp (125, 150 or 175 W) for at least 45 minutes.
3. Sit quietly for 5-15 minutes of recovery.

C. Incremental Aerobic Exercise to Maximum

1. Sit quietly for 3 minutes. When gas analysis data indicates relaxation and a true resting state, 3 minutes of resting data are obtained. Gas analysis is continuous from that point.
2. Walk on the treadmill at 3.5 $mi\cdot hr^{-1}$ at 0% grade for 1 minute. Continue to maximal exertion:

- Treadmill grade is elevated 2% after the first minute.
- Treadmill grade is elevated 1% per minute each minute until 22% grade.
- Treadmill speed remains constant at 3.5 $mi\cdot hr^{-1}$ until 22% grade when speed is increased 0.5 $mi\cdot hr^{-1}$ every minute.
- On a cycle ergometer, pedal at 1 kp at 50 $rev\cdot min^{-1}$ (50 W) for 2 minutes. The workrate is then increased by 0.5 kp (25 W) every 2 minutes until volitional fatigue.

3. Cool down by walking or pedaling lightly for 3 minutes.
4. Sit quietly for 5-15 minutes of recovery.

D. Static Exercise

Note to Instructor: A handgrip dynamometer or an adjustable two-leg extension is recommended.

1. Sit quietly for 3 minutes. When gas analysis data indicates relaxation and a true resting state, 3 minutes of resting data are obtained. Gas analysis is continuous from that point.
2. Contract maximally for 2 minutes: Be sure to give a maximal effort from the start, but avoid performing the Valsalva maneuver.
3. Sit quietly for 5-15 minutes of recovery.

E. Constant Load Dynamic Resistance Exercise

Note to Instructor: Pre-testing for 1 RM should either be completed sufficiently ahead of time to allow full recovery, or a student selected who knows his/her 1 RM

1. Sit quietly for 3 minutes. When gas analysis data indicates relaxation and a true resting state, 3 minutes of resting data are obtained. Gas analysis is continuous from that point.
2. Perform 4 sets of 10-12 repetitions at 75% 1 RM of 1-arm biceps curl or two-leg extension, resting 1 minute between sets: Be sure to give a maximal effort, but avoid performing the Valsalva maneuver.
3. Sit quietly for 5-15 minutes of recovery.

Student Activities I
Analysis of Respiratory Responses to Different Categories of Exercise.

A. Definitions.

Define the following key terms. For those terms which are measurable variables, describe in your own words what they mean (not how they are obtained or calculated). Indicate the unit(s) of measurement.

1. Alveolar Ventilation (V_A):

2. Exercise Response:

3. Frequency (f):

4. Minute Ventilation (V_E):

5. Respiration:

6. Tidal Volume (V_T):

7. Training Adaptations:

B. Analysis.

1. Using the variables V_E, V_T, and f, prepare a separate graph for each category of exercise. You should have 5 graphs for each variable if all categories of exercise were performed. See examples of different types of graphs on pages 12-14. For the dynamic resistance exercise, be sure to indicate the rest periods between sets on the X-axis.

C. Interpretation and Discussion.

1. Describe the pattern of response seen for each of the respiratory variables during each category of exercise. Compare and contrast your results for each variable with expected patterns. Explain any variations from the expected patterns.

2. Depending upon which data you have available, compare and contrast the male/female responses or the responses based on training status. If you do not have data, do a theoretical analysis of one of these.

3. Discuss the neural factors that control the respiratory response to various categories of exercise.

4. For those categories of exercise where information is available, describe what should happen to arterial partial pressure of oxygen (PaO_2), venous partial pressure of oxygen (PvO_2) and venous partial pressure of carbon dioxide ($PvCO_2$).

D. Application.

1. Defend or Refute: Maximal, dynamic, rythmical exercise is limited by the capacity of the respiratory system.

Related Readings

1. Plowman, S.A. & Smith, D.L. (2003). Exercise Physiology for Health, Fitness and Performance (2nd ed.). San Fransisco: Benjamin Cummings.
2. Powers, S.K. & Howley, E.T. (2001). Exercise Physiology: Theory and Application to Fitness and Performance (4th ed.) (pp. 200-207). Boston: McGraw-Hill.
3. McArdle, W.D., Katch, F.I. & Katch, V.L. (2001). Exercise Physiology: Energy, Nutrition and Human Performance (5th ed.) (290-297, 299-300). Baltimore: Williams & Wilkins.

Student Activities II
Analysis of Cardiovascular Responses to Different Categories of Exercise

A. Definitions.

Define the following key terms. For those terms which are measurable variables, describe in your own words what they mean (not how they are obtained or calculated). Indicate the unit(s) of measurement.

1. Diastolic Blood Pressure (DBP):

2. Heart Rate (HR):

3. Incremental Exercise to Maximum:

4. Long-Term, Moderate to Heavy Submaximal Aerobic Exercise:

5. Mean Arterial Pressure (MAP):

6. Pulse Pressure (PP):

7. Rate Pressure Product (RPP):

8. Short-Term, Light to Moderate Submaximal Aerobic Exercise:

9. Systolic Blood Pressure (SBP):

B. Analysis.

1. Using the following formulas, calculate MAP and PP for each category of exercise tested for each minute where data is available:

   PP = SBP - DBP (use DBP_1 for exercise; DBP_2 for rest and recovery)
   MAP = 1/3 PP + DBP_2 (rest and recovery)
   MAP = 1/2 PP + DBP_1 (exercise)

2. Calculate RPP for each category of exercise tested using the following formula:

   RPP = [HR x SBP]/100 (RPP has no unit of measurement)

3. Using the variables HR, BP (SBP, DBP and MAP) and RPP, prepare a separate graph for each category of exercise. You should have 5 graphs for each variable if all categories of exercise were performed. See examples of different types of graphs on pages 12-14. For the dynamic resistance exercise, be sure to indicate the rest periods between sets on the X-axis.

C. Interpretation and Discussion.

1. Describe the pattern of response seen for each of the cardiovascular variables measured during each category of exercise. Compare and contrast your results for each variable with expected patterns. Explain any variations from the expected pattern.

2. Depending upon which data you have available, compare and contrast the male/female responses or the responses based on training status. If you do not have data, do a theoretical analysis of one of these.

3. Discuss the neural factors that control the cardiovascular response to various categories of exercise.

4. Physiologically, explain the necessity for the expected normal blood pressure responses to exercise and why there are differences between the various categories of exercise.

5. Defend or Refute: A different formula should be used to calculate MAP during exercise than during rest and recovery.

D. Application.

1. Defend or Refute: Dynamic resistance training causes hypertension.

Related Readings

1. Plowman, S.A. & Smith, D.L. (2003). Exercise Physiology for Health, Fitness and Performance (2nd ed.). San Fransisco: Benjamin Cummings.
2. Powers, S.K. & Howley, E.T. (2001). Exercise Physiology: Theory and Application to Fitness and Performance (4th ed.) (pp. 176-180). Boston: McGraw-Hill.
3. McArdle, W.D., Katch, F.I. & Katch, V.L. (2001). Exercise Physiology: Energy, Nutrition and Human Performance (5th ed.) (pp. 318-323, 347-355). Baltimore: Williams & Wilkins.

Student Actvities III

Analysis of Metabolic Responses to Different Categories of Exercise.

A. Definitions.

Define the following key terms. For those terms which are measurable variables, describe in your own words what they mean (not how they are obtained or caculated). Indicate the unit(s) of measurement.

1. Dynamic Resistance Exercise:

2. Excess Post-Exercise Oxygen Consumption (EPOC):

3. Lactate Concentration ($[La^-]$):

4. Oxygen Consumption (VO_2):

5. Rate of Perceived Exertion (RPE):

6. Respiratory Exchange Ratio (RER):

B. Analysis.

1. Using the variables VO_2, RPE, $[La^-]$ and RER, prepare a separate graph for each category of exercise. You should have 5 graphs for each variable if all categories of exercise were performed. See examples of different types of graphs on pages 12-14. For the dynamic resistance exercise, be sure to indicate the rest periods between sets on the X-axis.

C. Interpretation and Discussion.

1. Describe the pattern of response seen for each of the metabolic variables during each category of exercise. Compare and contrast your results for each variable with expected patterns. Explain any variations from the expected pattern.

2. Depending upon which data you have available, compare and contrast the male/female responses or the responses based on training status. If you do not have data, do a theoretical analysis of one of these.

3. Discuss the neurohormonal regulation of metabolism and how it is altered during exercise.

4. Rank order from highest to lowest a) the categories of exercise for O_2 deficit and b) the categories of exercise for EPOC.

D. Application.

1. Defend or Refute: The most effective way to lose body fat is long duration, low intensity aerobic exercise.

Related Readings

1. Plowman, S.A. & Smith, D.L. (2003). Exercise Physiology for Health, Fitness and Performance (2nd ed.). San Fransisco: Benjamin Cummings.
2. Powers, S.K. & Howley, E.T. (2001). Exercise Physiology: Theory and Application to Fitness and Performance (4th ed.) (pp. 48-62). Boston: McGraw-Hill.
3. McArdle, W.D., Katch, F.I. & Katch, V.L. (2001). Exercise Physiology: Energy, Nutrition and Human Performance (5th ed.) (pp. 158-163, 165-172). Baltimore: Williams & Wilkins.

Data Table 1.0: Short-Term, Light to Moderate Submaximal Aerobic Exercise

Name: ______________________ Age (yr): ____________ Temp (°C): ____________

Training Status: ______________________ Ht (cm): ____________ P_B (mmHg): ____________

Sex: ______________________ Wt (kg): ____________ RH (%): ____________

	Time (minutes)	V_E ($L \cdot min^{-1}$)	f ($b \cdot min^{-1}$)	V_T ($L \cdot br^{-1}$)	HR ($b \cdot min^{-1}$)	BP (mmHg)	RPE	VO_2 ($L \cdot min^{-1}$)	RER	$[La^-]$ ($mmol \cdot L^{-1}$)
Rest	1									
	2									
	3									
Exercise	1									
	2									
	3									
	4									
	5									
	6									
	7									
	8									
	9									
	10									
Recovery	1									
	2									
	3									
	4									
	5									
	6									
	7									
	8									
	9									
	10									
	11									
	12									
	13									
	14									
	15									

Data Table 2.0: Long-Term, Moderate to Heavy Submaximal Aerobic Exercise

Name: ______________________ Age (yr): __________ Temp (°C): __________

Training Status: ______________________ Ht (cm): __________ P_B (mmHg): __________

Sex: ______________________ Wt (kg): __________ RH (%): __________

	Time (minutes)	V_E ($L \cdot min^{-1}$)	f ($b \cdot min^{-1}$)	V_T ($L \cdot br^{-1}$)	HR ($b \cdot min^{-1}$)	BP (mmHg)	RPE	VO_2 ($L \cdot min^{-1}$)	RER	$[La^-]$ ($mmol \cdot L^{-1}$)
Rest	1									
	2									
	3									
Exercise	1									
	2									
	3									
	4									
	5									
	6									
	7									
	8									
	9									
	10									
	11									
	12									
	13									
	14									
	15									
	16									
	17									
	18									
	19									
	20									
	21									
	22									
	23									
	24									
	25									
	26									
	27									
	28									
	29									

	Time (minutes)	V_E ($L \cdot min^{-1}$)	f ($b \cdot min^{-1}$)	V_T ($L \cdot br^{-1}$)	HR ($b \cdot min^{-1}$)	BP (mmHg)	RPE	VO_2 ($L \cdot min^{-1}$)	RER	$[La^-]$ ($mmol \cdot L^{-1}$)
	30									
	31									
	32									
	33									
	34									
	35									
	36									
	37									
	38									
	39									
	40									
	41									
	42									
	43									
	44									
	45									
Recovery	1									
	2									
	3									
	4									
	5									
	6									
	7									
	8									
	9									
	10									
	11									
	12									
	13									
	14									
	15									

Data Table 3.0: Incremental Aerobic Exercise to Maximum

Name: ______________________ Age (yr): __________ Temp (°C): __________

Training Status: ______________________ Ht (cm): __________ P_B (mmHg): __________

Sex: ______________________ Wt (kg): __________ RH (%): __________

	Time (minutes)	V_E ($L \cdot min^{-1}$)	f ($b \cdot min^{-1}$)	V_T ($L \cdot br^{-1}$)	HR ($b \cdot min^{-1}$)	BP (mmHg)	RPE	VO_2 ($L \cdot min^{-1}$)	RER	[La^-] ($mmol \cdot L^{-1}$)
Rest	1									
	2									
	3									
Exercise	1									
	2									
	3									
	4									
	5									
	6									
	7									
	8									
	9									
	10									
	11									
	12									
	13									
	14									
	15									
	16									
	17									
	18									
	19									
	20									
	21									
	22									
	23									
	24									
	25									
	26									
	27									
	28									
	29									

	Time (minutes)	V_E (L·min^{-1})	f (b·min^{-1})	V_T (L·br^{-1})	HR (b·min^{-1})	BP (mmHg)	RPE	VO_2 (L·min^{-1})	RER	[La$^-$] (mmol·L^{-1})
	30									
Recovery	1									
	2									
	3									
	4									
	5									
	6									
	7									
	8									
	9									
	10									
	11									
	12									
	13									
	14									
	15									

Data Table 4.0: Static Exercise

Name:	______________	Age (yr):	______	Temp (°C):	______
Training Status:	______________	Ht (cm):	______	P_B (mmHg):	______
Sex:	______________	Wt (kg):	______	RH (%):	______

	Time (minutes)	V_E (L·min^{-1})	f (b·min^{-1})	V_T (L·br^{-1})	HR (b·min^{-1})	BP* (mmHg)	RPE	VO_2 (L·min^{-1})	RER	[La$^-$] (mmol·L^{-1})
Rest	1									
	2									
	3									
Exercise	.5									
	1.0									
	1.5									
	2.0									
Recovery	1									
	2									
	3									
	4									
	5									
	6									
	7									
	8									
	9									
	10									
	11									
	12									
	13									
	14									
	15									

* *Note: It is very difficult to take blood pressure measurements during static exercise. Here are a few suggestions to ensure better blood pressure measurements.*

- *Have the most experienced person collect blood pressure data.*
- *Place the blood pressure cuff on the non-exercising arm; either arm will do if leg exercise is being done.*
- *Remind the subject to relax the non-exercising arm or arms.*
- *Start inflating the blood pressure cuff early so that the measurement is obtained by the desired time point.*

Data Table 5.0: Dynamic Resistance Exercise

Name: ______________________ Age (yr): __________ Temp (°C): __________

Training Status: ______________________ Ht (cm): __________ P_B (mmHg): __________

Sex: ______________________ Wt (kg): __________ RH (%): __________

	Time (minutes)	V_E ($L \cdot min^{-1}$)	f ($b \cdot min^{-1}$)	V_T ($L \cdot br^{-1}$)	HR ($b \cdot min^{-1}$)	BP (mmHg)	RPE	VO_2 ($L \cdot min^{-1}$)	RER	[La^-] ($mmol \cdot L^{-1}$)
Rest	1									
	2									
	3									
Exercise	Set 1									
	Rest									
	Set 2									
	Rest									
	Set 3									
	Rest									
	Set 4									
Recovery	1									
	2									
	3									
	4									
	5									
	6									
	7									
	8									
	9									
	10									
	11									
	12									
	13									
	14									
	15									

Lactate Responses

Anaerobic, Aerobic Endurance and Resistance Exercise

Student Learning Objectives

After completing this lab, you should be able to:

1. Define, explain and correctly use key terms.
2. Describe the lactate response to anaerobic, aerobic and resistance exercise.
3. Calculate peak power, mean power and fatigue index from the 30 Second Wingate Anaerobic Test (WAT).

Equipment

- Barbells (up to 120 lbs./54.5 kg)
- Wingate Computer Program (optional)
- Cones/Tape Measure (or 20 m marked course)
- Cycle Ergometer (modified to automatically count revolutions every second)
- Heart Rate Watches/Transmitter Straps
- Lactate Analyzer and Accessories
- Stopwatch

Procedure

The lactate responses to anaerobic, aerobic and resistance exercise will be examined. A different student should perform each protocol with lactate measured before and after. As many of the remaining students in the lab section as possible should perform either the 30 Second WAT or the Field Anaerobic Shuttle Test (FAST) with or without lactate measurement. Any student doing protocols B, D or E and meeting the weight limitation who also wishes to do the 30 Second WAT may do so, but only after his/her primary protocol. Many cycle ergometers cannot tolerate the power exerted by very large muscular trained individuals; therefore, a 200 lb. weight limit is suggested for selecting students to perform the 30 Second WAT.

Note to Student: Make sure you eat a light snack, but not a full meal, before this experiment.

Protocols

A. The 30 Second Wingate Anaerobic Test (WAT)[1]

1. Obtain a pre-exercise lactate measurement and record in Data Table 1.0.
2. Calculate the resistance you must pedal against by multiplying your body weight in kilograms by 0.075.
3. Warm up by riding the cycle ergometer for 5 minutes at a heart rate of 150 $b \cdot min^{-1}$, interspersing several short but intense accelerations for 5-10 seconds.
4. Rest for 3 minutes.
5. Begin the test by pedaling as fast as possible.
6. A partner applies the calculated resistance when maximum pedal revolutions are attained.
7. Continue to pedal as fast as possible for 30 seconds.

Note to Instructor: An automated count of revolutions per second is recommended (hand calculations may be inaccurate). Revolutions should be counted for exactly 30 seconds. Use Data Table 2.0 if a manual count is made.

8. Cool down by pedaling against a light resistance for 3 minutes.
9. Obtain a post-exercise lactate measurement and record in Data Table 1.0.

B. 10 Second Wingate Speed Test (WST)

1. Obtain a pre-exercise lactate measurement and record in Data Table 1.0.
2. Warm up by riding the cycle ergometer for 5 minutes at a heart rate of 150 b·min^{-1}, interspersing several short but intense accelerations for 5-10 seconds.
3. Rest for 3 minutes.
4. Begin test by pedaling as fast as possible.
5. A partner applies a load of 1 kg when maximum pedal revolutions are attained.
6. Continue to pedal as fast as possible for 10 seconds.
7. Cool down by pedaling against a light resistance for 3 minutes.
8. Obtain a post-exercise lactate measurement and record in Data Table 1.0.

C. Field Anaerobic Shuttle Test (FAST)[2]

1. Mark off two lines 20 meters apart with tape or cones.
2. Obtain a pre-exercise lactate measurement and record in Data Table 1.0.
3. Warm up by jogging between the two lines/ cones for 5 minutes, gradually increasing speed.
4. Rest for 3 minutes.
5. Stand at one end of the 20 meter shuttle course.
6. Run as fast as possible 6 times back and forth for a total of 12 lengths (240 m).
7. Cool down by walking for 3 minutes.
8. Obtain a post-exercise lactate measurement and record in Data Table 1.0.

D. 20 Minute Submaximal Cycle Ergometer Ride (20 min.)

1. Obtain a pre-exercise lactate measurement and record in Data Table 1.0.
2. Ride the cycle ergometer for 20 minutes at a heart rate $\leq$ 135 b·min^{-1}.
3. Cool down by pedaling against a light resistance for 3 minutes.
4. Obtain a post-exercise lactate measurement and record in Data Table 1.0.

E. Dynamic Resistance Exercise (Resistance)

1. Obtain a pre-exercise lactate measurement and record in Data Table 1.0.
2. Perform 4 sets of a two-arm biceps curl using a weight equivalent to your 10-15 repetition maximum, resting 1 minute between sets.
3. Cool down by lifting a light load (i.e., just the weight bar) for 3 minutes.
4. Obtain a post-exercise lactate measurement and record in Data Table 1.0.

Data Table 1.0

	WAT	WST	FAST	20 min.	Resistance
Pre $[La^-]$					
Post $[La^-]$					
Post-Pre $[La^-]$					

Data Table 2.0

Name: ________________

Weight: ________________

Resistance for Legs: ________

Revolutions·5 s^{-1} Manual Count

Time (s)	Revolutions
1-5	
6-10	
11-15	
16-20	
21-25	
26-30	
Total Revolutions	

Data Table 3.0*

Subject	Sex	PP (W)	PP (W) Clf	PP ($W \cdot kg^{-1}$)	PP ($W \cdot kg^{-1}$) Clf	MP (W)	MP (W) Clf	MP ($W \cdot kg^{-1}$)	MP ($W \cdot kg^{-1}$) Clf	FI (%)	FI Clf
1											
2											
3											
4											
5											
6											
7											
8											
9											
10											
11											
12											
13											
14											
15											
16											
17											
18											
19											
20											
Mean											
SD											

* *Abbreviations: Clf, Classification. FI, Fatigue Index. PP, Peak Power. MP, Mean Power.. W, Watts.*

Box 1.0

Name:	Sally Fit	Total Pedal Revolutions:	50.25 revs
Weight:	70.75 kg	Highest Revolutions·5 s^{-1}:	10.5 revs
Resistance for Legs:	5.3 kg	Lowest Revolutions·5 s^{-1}:	6.25 revs
		Distance the Flywheel Travels:	6 $m \cdot rev^{-1}$

a. <u>Peak Power (PP)</u>

- Identify highest revolutions·5 s^{-1}; usually, this is seconds 1-5 or 2-6.
- PP ($kgm \cdot 5\ s^{-1}$) = Resistance for Legs x Highest Revolutions·5 s^{-1} x Distance the Flywheel Travels
- Convert PP $kgm \cdot 5\ s^{-1}$ to $kgm \cdot min^{-1}$ by multiplying $kgm \cdot 5\ s^{-1}$ by 12.
- Convert $kgm \cdot min^{-1}$ to watts (W) by dividing $kgm \cdot min^{-1}$ by 6.12 (1 W = 6.12 $kgm \cdot min^{-1}$).

Sally Fit Example:

PP ($kgm \cdot 5\ s^{-1}$) = 5.3 x 10.5 x 6 = 333.9 $kgm \cdot 5\ s^{-1}$
PP ($kgm \cdot min^{-1}$) = 333.9 $kgm \cdot 5\ s^{-1}$ x 12 = 4006.8 $kgm \cdot min^{-1}$
PP (W) = 4006.8 $kgm \cdot min^{-1}$ ÷ 6.12 $kgm \cdot min^{-1} \cdot W^{-1}$ = 654.7 W

b. <u>Peak Power Relative to Body Weight (PP·BW)</u>

- PP·BW ($kgm \cdot min^{-1} \cdot kg^{-1}$) = PP ($kgm \cdot min^{-1}$) ÷ BW (kg)
- PP·BW ($W \cdot kg^{-1}$) = PP (W) ÷ BW (kg)

Sally Fit Example:

PP·BW ($kgm \cdot min^{-1} \cdot kg^{-1}$) = 4006.8 $kgm \cdot min^{-1}$ ÷ 70.75 kg = 56.63 $kgm \cdot min^{-1} \cdot kg^{-1}$
PP·BW ($W \cdot kg^{-1}$) = 654.7 W ÷ 70.75 kg = 9.25 $W \cdot kg^{-1}$

c. <u>Mean Power (MP)</u>

- MP ($kgm \cdot 30\ s^{-1}$) = Total Pedal Revolutions x Resistance for Legs x Distance the Flywheel Travels
- Calculate total pedal revolutions by adding up the revolutions for intervals 1-5 + 6-10 + 11-15 + 16-20 + 21-25 + 26-30.
- Convert $kgm \cdot 30\ s^{-1}$ to $kgm \cdot min^{-1}$ by multiplying $kgm \cdot 30\ s^{-1}$ by 2.
- Convert $kgm \cdot min^{-1}$ to watts (W) by dividing $kgm \cdot min^{-1}$ by 6.12 (1 watt =6.12 $kgm \cdot min^{-1}$).

Sally Fit Example:

MP ($kgm \cdot 30\ s^{-1}$) = 50.25 x 5.3 x 6 = 1597.95 $kgm \cdot 30\ s^{-1}$
MP ($kgm \cdot min^{-1}$) = 1597.95 $kgm \cdot 30\ s^{-1}$ x 2 = 3195.9 $kgm \cdot min^{-1}$
MP (W) = 3195.9 $kgm \cdot min^{-1}$ ÷ 6.12 $kgm \cdot min^{-1} \cdot W^{-1}$ = 522.2 W

d. <u>Mean Power Relative to Body Weight (MP·BW)</u>

- Calculate MP·BW = MP ($kgm \cdot min^{-1}$) ÷ BW (kg)
- Convert $kgm \cdot min^{-1} \cdot kg^{-1}$ to watts (W) by dividing $kgm \cdot min^{-1} \cdot kg^{-1}$ by 6.12 (1 watt =6.12 $kgm \cdot min^{-1}$).

Sally Fit Example:

MP·BW ($kgm \cdot min^{-1} \cdot kg^{-1}$) = 3195.9 $kgm \cdot min^{-1}$ ÷ 70.75 kg = 45.17 $kgm \cdot min^{-1} \cdot kg^{-1}$
MP·BW ($W \cdot kg^{-1}$) = 45.17 $kgm \cdot min^{-1} \cdot kg^{-1}$ ÷ 6.12 $kgm \cdot min^{-1} \cdot W^{-1}$ = 7.38 $W \cdot kg^{-1}$

e. <u>Fatigue Index (FI)</u>

- Fatigue index can be calculated using either equation 1 or 2.

$$1)\quad FI = \left[\frac{\text{highest 5 s power} - \text{lowest 5 s power}}{\text{highest 5 s power}}\right] \times 100 \qquad 2)\quad FI = \left[1.0 - \frac{\text{lowest 5 s power}}{\text{highest 5 s power}}\right] \times 100$$

- Highest 5 s power = PP ($kgm \cdot 5\ s^{-1}$)
- Identify lowest number of revolutions·5 s^{-1}; usually, this is seconds 21-25 or 26-30.
- Lowest 5 s Power ($kgm \cdot 5\ s^{-1}$) = Resistance for Legs x Lowest Revolutions·5 s^{-1} x Distance the Flywheel Travels

Sally Fit Example:

Highest 5 s Power = 333.9 $kgm \cdot 5\ s^{-1}$
Lowest 5 s Power ($kgm \cdot 5\ s^{-1}$) = 5.3 x 6.25 x 6 = 198.75 $kgm \cdot 5\ s^{-1}$

$$1)\quad FI = \left[\frac{333.9\ kgm \cdot 5\ s^{-1} - 198.75\ kgm \cdot 5\ s^{-1}}{333.9\ kgm \cdot 5\ s^{-1}}\right] \times 100 = 40.48\% \qquad 2)\quad FI = \left[1.0 - \frac{198.75\ kgm \cdot 5\ s^{-1}}{333.9\ kgm \cdot 5\ s^{-1}}\right] \times 100 = 40.48\%$$

Student Activities

A. Definitions.

Define the following key terms. For those terms which are measureable variables, describe in your own words what they mean (not how they are obtained or calculated). Indicate the unit(s) of measurement.

1. Fatigue Index:

2. Glycogen:

3. Fast Glycolysis:

4. Lactic Acid:

5. Mean Power:

6. Peak Power:

7. pH:

8. Phospahgen:

9. Triglyceride:

B. Analysis.

1. Using the data from the 30 second WAT printout or Data Table 2.0, calculate the following variables (formulas for calculating each variable can be found in Box 1.0; classification information can be found in Appendix A):

   a. Peak Power ($kgm{\cdot}min^{-1}$ and watts) for the highest 5 second interval
   b. Peak Power Relative to Body Weight ($kgm{\cdot}min^{-1}{\cdot}kg^{-1}$ and $watts{\cdot}kg^{-1}$) for the highest 5 second interval
   c. Mean Power for 30 seconds
   d. Mean Power Relative to Body Weight for 30 seconds
   e. Fatigue Index

   Complete Data Table 3.0 for yourself and/or classmates as directed by your instructor.

2. Prepare a bar graph using the pre-exercise lactate values and the 3-minute post-exercise lactate values for the 30 Second WAT, 10 Second WST, FAST, 20 Minute Submaximal Cycle Ergometer Ride and the Dynamic Resistance Exercise.

C. Interpretation and Discussion.

1. Discuss the peak power, mean power and the fatigue index results.

2. Compare and contrast the lactate response to the 30 Second WAT, 10 Second WST, FAST, 20 Minute Submaximal Cycle Ergometer Ride and Dynamic Resistance Exercise. Do the lab values agree with the normal expected range reported based on high intensity exercise times?

3. Defend or Refute: Lactate accumulation results from a lack of oxygen.

D. Application.

1. Describe the expected lactic acid/lactate responses to the following exercise situations. Defend your response.

- 8 minute basketball quarter
- 3 minute hockey shift
- 45 minute soccer half (not goal keeper)
- 1500 meter swim
- triple jump

References

1. Bar-Or, O. (1987). The Wingate Anaerobic Test: An update on methodology, reliability and validity. Sports Medicine, 4, 381-394.
2. Thomas, C., Plowman, S.A., & Looney, M.A. Reliability and validity of a laboratory and a field test for measuring anaerobic work capacity in soccer players. Measurement in Physical Education and Exercise Science (In Press).

Related Readings

1. Plowman, S.A. & Smith, D.L. (2003). Exercise Physiology for Health, Fitness and Performance (2nd ed.). San Fransisco: Benjamin Cummings.
2. Powers, S.K. & Howley, E.T. (2001). Exercise Physiology: Theory and Application to Fitness and Performance (4th ed.) (pp. 51-55, 398-399). Boston: McGraw-Hill.
3. McArdle, W.D., Katch, F.I. & Katch, V.L. (2001). Exercise Physiology: Energy, Nutrition and Human Performance (5th ed.) (pp. 158-160, 290-296). Baltimore: Williams & Wilkins.

Power Output: Field Tests

Vertical Jump and Step Tests

Student Learning Objectives

After completing this lab, you should be able to:

1. Define, explain and correctly use key terms.
2. Describe how aerobic power and anaerobic power can be estimated from step tests.
3. Explain the relationship between power output, energy expenditure and exercise intensity.
4. Distinguish between field tests and criterion tests for measuring power output.

Equipment

- Heart Rate Watches/Transmitter Straps
- Measuring Tape (or other means of assessing vertical jump)
- Metronome/Stopwatch
- Step Bench (≈ 40 cm for females; 50 cm for males)

Procedure

Anaerobic power will be estimated from a vertical jump test, and two step tests will be used to estimate aerobic and anaerobic power. All students will be subjects; students should work with a partner and test each other.

Protocols

Before doing the vertical jump and step tests, warm up using the following routine:

1. Walk in place at a moderate pace for 2 minutes, lifting knees to the waist or higher.
2. Statically stretch the calves, quadriceps, groin and hamstrings.
3. Practice the stepping pattern of the two step tests at a moderate pace for 2 minutes.
4. Actively recover by either walking or stretching for 2 minutes.

A. <u>Vertical Jump Test</u>

1. Fasten measuring tape to wall or adjust jump standard.
2. Stand facing the measuring tape with your toes touching the wall and reach up: A partner reads the tape and records the standing height to the nearest 0.5 inch in Data Table 1.0.
3. Turn your side to the wall; without taking a step, jump as high as possible, tapping the measuring tape with your inside hand: Your partner stands on a bench to read the jumping height at eye level and records in Data Table 1.0.
4. Rest for 30 seconds.
5. Repeat steps 2 and 3 two more times.
6. Calculate vertical jump by subtracting the standing height from jumping height, and use the highest value for classification analysis (*Appendix A*).

Data Table 1.0			
Jumping Height	____ (cm/in)	____ (cm/in)	____ (cm/in)
Standing Height	____ (cm/in)	____ (cm/in)	____ (cm/in)
Vertical Jump	____ (cm/in)	____ (cm/in)	____ (cm/in)
Highest Vertical Jump	____ (cm/in)		
Classification	____		

B. Aerobic Power Step Test (AP)[4]: California State University, Long beach Step Test (CSULB)

1. Put on a heart rate monitor.
2. Measure the height of the bench, in centimeters and meters, and your weight with shoes and record in Data Table 2.0.
3. Select a stepping pace based on your VO_2 max (this estimate can be determined from the treadmill VO_2 max, PACER or non-exercise questionnaire VO_2 max):

- <40 $mL \cdot kg^{-1} \cdot min^{-1}$ (24 $steps \cdot min^{-1}$)
- 40-55 $mL \cdot kg^{-1} \cdot min^{-1}$ (30 $steps \cdot min^{-1}$)
- >55 $mL \cdot kg^{-1} \cdot min^{-1}$ (36 $steps \cdot min^{-1}$)

> *Note to Student: The heart rate attained during exercise should be between 145 and 170 $b \cdot min^{-1}$ for valid results. Make sure spacing between subjects is sufficient so that heart rate watches do not interfere with each other.*

4. Step at the pre-determined rate for 3 minutes, stepping in the traditional up-up, down-down pattern where one leg and then the other is raised up on the bench and down again. Your back should remain straight throughout the test and you should fully extend both legs during the up phase.
5. Your partner counts the number of steps completed in 3 minutes and records in Data Table 2.0.
6. Read your heart rate during the last 10 seconds of stepping and record in Data Table 2.0. If no heart rate monitor is available, measure your heart rate for 15 seconds immmediately after exercise and use the following formula[4] to estimate your exercise heart rate:

Exercise HR = 16.32 + (3.72 x 15 s count)
16.32 + (3.72 x ______) = ______ $b \cdot min^{-1}$

Data Table 2.0	
Weight (kg)	
Bench Height (cm and m)	
Total # of Steps	
Heart Rate ($b \cdot min^{-1}$)	

C. Anaerobic Power Step Test (AnP)[1,3]

1. Measure the bench height, in centimeters and meters, and your weight with shoes and record in Data Table 3.0.
2. Stand perpendicular to the bench. Place the foot of your test leg (choose left or right) on the bench surface and the other foot flat on the floor. Keep your back straight and your arms at the side.
3. Complete as many repetitions as possible in 1 minute, raising your body to the top of the step with the test leg while the other leg dangles.

> *Note: The legs and back must be kept straight. The arms can be used for balance, but not for momentum (i.e., no pumping). Do not bounce back from the floor; the stress should be on the quadriceps, not the calf muscles. Be sure the foot of the test leg is flat on the bench. No pacing.*

4. Your partner counts each complete up-down step as up-1, up-2, up-3, etc., the number designating the down portion of the step.
5. Record the number of steps completed in 15, 30, and 60 seconds in Data Table 3.0

Data Table 3.0	
Weight (kg)	
Bench Height (cm and m)	
Number of Steps	
15 seconds	
30 seconds	
60 seconds	

Data Table 4.0

Subject	Sex	Anaerobic Power (W)			Aerobic Power		PACER VO_2 max	Measured VO_2 max Treadmill Test*
		Vertical Jump	Step Tests 15 s	Step Tests 30 s	Watts	$mL \cdot kg^{-1} \cdot min^{-1}$	$mL \cdot kg^{-1} \cdot min^{-1}$	$mL \cdot kg^{-1} \cdot min^{-1}$
1								
2								
3								
4								
5								
6								
7								
8								
9								
10								
11								
12								
13								
14								
15								
16								
17								
18								
19								
20								
Mean								
SD								

* *Note: Only students who were also subjects for the Maximal Oxygen Consumption lab will have data for this column.*

Student Activities

A. Definitions.

Define the following key terms. For those terms which are measurable variables, describe in your own words what they mean (not how they are obtained or calculated). Indicate the unit(s) of measurement.

1. Aerobic Power (AP):

2. Anaerobic Power (AnP):

3. Power:

B. Analysis.

1. Calculate AnP from the vertical jump using the following formula:[2]

   AnP (kgm·sec^{-1}) = (sq. root of 4.9 x BW x sq. root of VJ)

   Where the sq. root of 4.9 = 2.21359, BW = body weight in kg and VJ = height jumped in meters

   For example: A student weighs 68 kg and has a vertical jump of 16 inches.

   AnP = 2.21359 x 68 kg x sq. root of .4064 m
   AnP = 2.21359 x 68 kg x .6439 m
   AnP = 95.95839 kgm·sec^{-1}

   To convert to watts, multiply kgm·sec^{-1} by 9.81

   AnP (W) = 95.95839 kgm·sec^{-1} x 9.81 = 941.35 W

2. Using the data in Data Table 2.0, calculate AP using the following formula:[4]

$$AP\ (kgm\cdot min^{-1}) = Force \times \frac{Distance}{time}$$

$$AP\ (kgm\cdot min^{-1}) = BW \times \frac{Number\ of\ Steps}{3} \times BH \times 1.35$$

Where BH = bench height in meters and BW = body weight in kg

For example: A student weighs 68 kg and performs 80 steps in 3 minutes on a bench 0.4 m high.

$$AP = 68\ kg \times \frac{80\ steps}{3} \times 0.4\ m \times 1.35$$

$$AP = 979.2\ kgm\cdot min^{-1}$$

To convert to watts, divide $kgm\cdot min^{-1}$ by $6.12\ kgm\cdot min^{-1}\cdot W^{-1}$.

$$AP(W) = 979.2\ kgm\cdot min^{-1} \div 6.12\ kgm\cdot min^{-1}\cdot watt = 160\ W$$

3. Estimate VO_2 max ($L\cdot min^{-1}$) using your estimated AP, your exercise heart rate during the AP test and one of the following VO_2 prediction equations based on your sex.[4]

VO_2 max Prediction Formulas:

Females: $VO_2\ max\ (L\cdot min^{-1}) = 6.85591 + 0.00368\ (AP) - 0.04338\ (HR)$
Males: $VO_2\ max\ (L\cdot min^{-1}) = 6.49104 + 0.00346\ (AP) - 0.04220\ (HR)$

For example: A female student had a heart rate of 158 $b\cdot min^{-1}$ and an AP of 979.2 $kgm\cdot min^{-1}$.

$$VO_2\ max = 6.85591 + 0.00368\ (979.2) - 0.04338\ (158)$$
$$VO_2\ max = 3.6\ L\cdot min^{-1}$$

4. Convert VO_2 max ($L \cdot min^{-1}$) from question 3 to $mL \cdot kg^{-1} \cdot min^{-1}$ by multiplying by 1000 and dividing by body weight in kg.

5. Using the data from Data Table 3.0, calculate peak anaerobic power (AnP_{peak}) for 15 and 30 seconds using the following formula:[1,3]

$$AnP_{peak}\ (kgm \cdot s^{-1}) = \frac{(F \times D)}{t} \times 1.33$$

Where F = weight of the subject in kg, D = height of bench in meters x number of steps in time period and t = time (sec)

For example: A student who weighs 68 kg steps up and down on a bench 0.4 m high and completes 17 steps in 15 seconds.

$$AnP_{peak} = \frac{(68 \times 0.4 \times 17)}{15} \times 1.33$$

$$AnP_{peak} = \frac{462.4}{15} \times 1.33$$

$$AnP_{peak} = 30.83 \times 1.33$$

$$AnP_{peak} = 40.99\ kgm \cdot s^{-1}$$

To convert to watts multiply $kgm \cdot s^{-1} \times 9.81$

$$AnP_{peak} = 40.99\ kgm \cdot s^{-1} \times 9.81 = 402.2\ W$$

C. Interpretation and Discussion.

1. Determine whether the tests listed below are aerobic or anaerobic tests. Then, determine whether the tests are field tests or criterion tests.

Test	Aerobic or Anaerobic	Field or Criterion
60 Second Step Test		
10 Second WST*		
3 Minute Step Test (CSULB)		
Non-Exercise Activity Questionnaire		
FAST		
30 Second WAT		
Vertical Jump		
Incremental Treadmill Test to Maximum		
PACER		
* <u>Note to Student</u>: *10 Second Wingate Speed Test from Lactate Responses lab.*		

2. Based on your personal data and/or the class data in Data Table 4.0, were the power outputs of the three field tests as expected relative to each other? Explain the physiological logic behind your answer.

3. Using your personal data and/or the class data in Data Table 4.0, compare the VO_2 max values calculated from the AP step test ($mL \cdot kg^{-1} \cdot min^{-1}$) to the PACER predicted VO_2 max and the VO_2 max measured during the *Maximal Oxygen Consumption* lab treadmill test. What might explain the differences, if any, between the VO_2 max values? Explain the impact of modality on measuring VO_2 max.

4. What is the relationship between power output, energy expenditure and exercise intensity?

D. Application.

1. For each test (Vertical Jump, Aerobic Power Step Test and Anaerobic Power Step Test), give 5 sports (specify position if needed) or events where this would give the most applicable information. Briefly justify your selections.

References

1. Adams, G.M., (1994). Exercise Physiology Laboratory Manual (2nd ed.) (pp. 73-78). Dubuque, IA: Wm. C. Brown.
2. Fox, E.L. & Matthews, D.K. (1974). Interval Training: Conditioning for Sports and General Fitness. Philidelphia: W.B. Saunders Co.
3. Manahan, J.E. & Gutin, B. (1971). The one-minute step test as a measure of 600 yard run performance. Research Quarterly, 42 (2), 173-177.
4. Mastropaolo, J., Bigelow, T.W., Takei, Y., Lugo, R. & Lyon, M.J. (1983). Training Manual for the Practice of Exercise Physiology (2nd ed.). Paramount, CA: Academy Printing & Publishing.

Related Readings

1. Plowman, S.A. & Smith, D.L. (2003). Exercise Physiology for Health, Fitness and Performance (2nd ed.). San Fransisco: Benjamin Cummings.
2. Powers, S.K. & Howley, E.T. (2001). Exercise Physiology: Theory and Application to Fitness and Performance (4th ed.) (pp. 395-399). Boston: McGraw-Hill.
3. McArdle, W.D., Katch, F.I. & Katch, V.L. (2001). Exercise Physiology: Energy, Nutrition and Human Performance (5th ed.) (pp. 224-231). Baltimore: Williams & Wilkins.

Caloric Cost and Efficiency

Impact of Body Weight or Simulated Altitude

Student Learning Objectives

After completing this lab, you should be able to:

1. Define, explain and correctly use key terms.
2. Explain how oxygen consumption (VO_2), respiratory exchange ratio (RER) and energy expenditue are related.
3. Calculate the caloric cost of an activity given VO_2, RER and duration of exercise.
4. Calculate delta efficiency given VO_2 for two steady state workrates.

Equipment

- Any Exercise Routine (6 minutes)
- Heart Rate Watches/Transmitter Straps
- Mats
- Weighted Vest, PO_2 Simulator or Specifically Mixed Gas for Inhalation (which simulates altitude)

Procedure

The relationship between VO_2, RER and energy expenditure will be examined using a 6-minute exercise routine with and without added body weight (or before and during altitude simulation). All students will be subjects.

Protocols

Note to Instructor: The Chicken Fat audio or video recording is a good exercise routine to use. A source for obtaining the video is included in Appendix B.

A. Control Condition

1. Put on a heart rate monitor.
2. Perform a 6-minute exercise routine.
3. Record heart rate (HR) each minute in Data Table 1.0 Control Condition if you were a VO_2 max subject for the *Maximal Oxygen Consumption* lab or Data Table 2.0 Control Condition if you were not.
4. Rest for 5 minutes.

B. Experimental Condition

1. Put on a heart rate monitor.
2. Repeat the 6-minute exercise routine under one of the following conditions:
   - Wearing a weighted vest with enough weight added to increase total body weight by 10%.
   - Wearing a PO_2 Aerobic Exerciser that simulates an altitude of ≈ 7500 ft.
   - Breathing from gas balloons that have been filled with an air mixture to simulate a selected altitude.
3. Record HR each minute in Data Table 1.0 Experimental Condition if you were a VO_2 max subject for the *Maximal Oxygen Consumption* lab or Data Table 2.0 Experimental Condition if you were not.

Data Table 1.0 VO_2 max Subject					
Control Condition					
Time (minutes)	HR ($b \cdot min^{-1}$)	VO_2 ($L \cdot min^{-1}$)	Caloric Equivalent ($kcal \cdot L\ O_2^{-1}$)	$kcals \cdot min^{-1}$	$kjoules \cdot min^{-1}$
1			5 kcals		
2			5 kcals		
3			5 kcals		
4			5 kcals		
5			5 kcals		
6			5 kcals		
			Total		
Experimental Condition					
Time (minutes)	HR ($b \cdot min^{-1}$)	VO_2 ($L \cdot min^{-1}$)	Caloric Equivalent ($kcal \cdot L\ O_2^{-1}$)	$kcals \cdot min^{-1}$	$kjoules \cdot min^{-1}$
1			5 kcals		
2			5 kcals		
3			5 kcals		
4			5 kcals		
5			5 kcals		
6			5 kcals		
			Total		

Data Table 1.0A *Maximal Oxygen Consumption* Data						
% VO_2 max	HR ($b \cdot min^{-1}$)	VO_2 ($L \cdot min^{-1}$)	RER	Caloric equivalent ($kcal \cdot L^{-1}\ O_2$)	$kcals \cdot min^{-1}$	$kjoules \cdot min^{-1}$
50						
65						
80						
95						
100						

Data Table 2.0
Non-VO_2 max Subject

Age (yr): _____	Resting HR ($b \cdot min^{-1}$): _________	PACER VO_2 max ($mL \cdot kg \cdot min^{-1}$): ___________
Weight (kg): _____	Maximal HR ($b \cdot min^{-1}$): _________	PACER VO_2R ($mL \cdot kg \cdot min^{-1}$):[a] ___________
		PACER VO_2R ($L \cdot min^{-1}$): ___________

Control Condition

Time (minutes)	HR ($b \cdot min^{-1}$)	% HRR[b]	% VO_2 R	VO_2[c] ($L \cdot min^{-1}$)	Caloric Equivalent (1 kcal·L O_2^{-1})	$kcals \cdot min^{-1}$
1					5 kcal	
2					5 kcal	
3					5 kcal	
4					5 kcal	
5					5 kcal	
6					5 kcal	
					Total	

Experimental Condition

Time (minutes)	HR ($b \cdot min^{-1}$)	% HRR	% VO_2R	VO_2 ($L \cdot min^{-1}$)	Caloric Equivalent (1 kcal·L O_2^{-1})	$kcals \cdot min^{-1}$
1					5 kcal	
2					5 kcal	
3					5 kcal	
4					5 kcal	
5					5 kcal	
6					5 kcal	
					Total	

Note to Student:

a. VO_2R ($mL \cdot kg \cdot min^{-1}$) = VO_2 max ($mL \cdot kg \cdot min^{-1}$) - VO_2 resting ($mL \cdot kg \cdot min^{-1}$)

b. *Heart Rate Reserve (HRR)* = $HR_{max} - HR_{rest}$

$$\% HRR = \frac{\text{Exercise Heart Rate } (b \cdot min^{-1}) - \text{Resting Heart Rate } (b \cdot min^{-1})}{\text{Heart Rate Reserve } (b \cdot min^{-1})}$$

$$\% HRR = \% VO_2R$$

c. $$VO_2 (L \cdot min^{-1}) = \% VO_2R\, [VO_2R\, (L \cdot min^{-1})] + \frac{3.5\ mL \cdot kg^{-1} \cdot min^{-1}}{\text{Body Weight (kg)}}$$

Box 1.0

Calculation of the Delta Efficiency of Walking on an Elevated Treadmill

Note to Student: For these computations, you will use the VO_2 L·min^{-1} values from the two 5 minute steady state walks collected during the maximal treadmill test conducted during the Maximal Oxygen Consumption: Criterion Test lab. Show all math.

Name of subject: ________________________ Weight of subject (to the nearest tenth of a kilogram): _______ kg

3.5 m·hr^{-1} 0% Grade Walk

1. Oxygen consumption during the 5 minute, 3.5 m·hr^{-1} 0% grade walk: _______L·min^{-1} (Average the 3rd, 4th and 5th minute).
2. Average RER value for the time period specified in #1: _______ (Average the 3rd, 4th and 5th minute).
3. Caloric equivalent based on the average RER value in #2: _______kcal·L^{-1} of O_2 (Usea table of caloric equivalencies).
4. Calculate kcal·min^{-1} by multiplying VO_2 in L·min^{-1} from step #1 by the caloric equivalent from step #3:

   _______L·min^{-1} x _______kcal·L^{-1} of O_2 = _______kcal·min^{-1}

3.5 m·hr^{-1} 10% Grade Walk

5. Oxygen consumption during the 5 minute, 3.5 mph 10 % grade walk _______ L·min^{-1} (Average the 3rd, 4th and 5th minute).
6. Average RER value for the time period specified in #5: _______ (Average the 3rd, 4th and 5th minute).
7. Caloric equivalent based on the average RER value in #6: _______ kcal·L^{-1} of O_2 (Use a table of caloric equivalencies).
8. Calculate kcal·min^{-1} by multiplying VO_2 in L·min^{-1} from step #5 by the caloric equivalent from step #7:

   _______ L·min^{-1} x _______ kcal·L^{-1} of O_2 = _______kcal·min^{-1}

Internal Cost of Elevated Walk

9. Subtract #4 from #8 to get the internal cost in kcal·min^{-1}:

   _______kcal·min^{-1} - _______kcal·min^{-1} = _______kcal·min^{-1}

External Cost of Elevated Walk

10. Estimate the caloric equivalent of the change in external power (P) of the walk and convert to kcal.

    a. P(kgm·min^{-1}) = [wt (kg) x speed in (m·min^{-1})] x (% slope ÷ 100)

    m·min^{-1} = mi·hr^{-1} x 26.8 = _______ x 26.8 = _______ m·min^{-1}

    P (kgm·min^{-1}) = [(_______kg x _______ m·min^{-1})] x (_______ ÷ 100) = _______)

    b. 1 kgm·min^{-1} = 0.00235 kcal

    _______kgm·min^{-1} (#10a) x 0.00235 = _______kcal. (This represents the external cost of the elevated walk).

Delta Efficiency (%)

11. Efficiency (%) = (External kcal ÷ Internal kcal) x 100

    (_______kcal ÷ _______ kcal) x 100 = _______%

Student Actvities

A. Definitions.

Define the following key terms. For those terms which are measurable variables, describe in your own words what they mean (not how they are obtained or calculated). Indicate the unit(s) of measurement.

1. Caloric Equivalent:

2. Calorie:

3. Economy:

4. Efficiency:

5. Intensity:

6. Respiratory Exchange Ratio (RER):

B. Analysis.

Note to Student: In order to complete the following analysis questions, you will need a subject's heart rate and oxygen consumption data from the Maximal Oxygen Consumption lab.

1. Using the VO_2 max subject's HR and VO_2 data from the *Maximal Oxygen Consumption* lab, graph HR versus VO_2 ($L \cdot min^{-1}$). Put HR on the Y-axis and VO_2 on the X-axis, and draw a line of best fit.

2. Using the line of best fit in the HR versus VO_2 graph, estimate the amount of O_2 consumed for each minute of the two, 6-minute exercise routines (Control and Experimental Conditions) for the VO_2 max subject (Data Table 1.0).

3. Using a table of caloric equivalencies and the data from the *Maximal Oxygen Consumption* lab, complete Data Table 1.0A for the VO_2 max subject. Calculate the energy expended (in kcals and kjoules) during the incremental treadmill test to maximum by multiplying O_2 consumption ($L \cdot min^{-1}$) by the caloric equivalent at the appropriate RER. Select minutes that represent approximately 50, 65, 80, 95 and 100% of VO_2 max.

4. Since there are no RER values for the VO_2 max subject's two, 6-minute exercise routines, estimate the caloric cost of the Control and Experimental Conditions (in kcals and kjoules) by using the caloric equivalent 1 liter of $O_2 \cdot min^{-1}$ equals 5 kcal (Data Table 1.0).

5. Complete Data Table 2.0 using the Non-VO_2 max subject's data and the known relationships between the other physiological variables.

6. Determine walking efficiency for the VO_2 max subject using Box 1.0.

C. Interpretation and Discussion.

1. From Data Table 1.0A, what happens to caloric cost as exercise intensity increases? What was the highest caloric expenditure the subject from the *Maximal Oxygen Consumption* lab was able to achieve?

2. What was the impact of excess weight or simulated altitude on the caloric cost of the 6-minute exercise routine for a) the VO_2 max subject and b) the Non-VO_2 max subject?

3. Compare and contrast the VO_2 max subject's calculated delta efficiency value with published data. Is it within normal expected range for treadmill walking? What would you expect to happen to efficiency if the subject gained weight or performed the activity at altitude?

D. Application.

1. In order to lose 1 lb. per week by exercise alone, how many times would the VO_2 max subject need to do the exercise routine a) without the added weight and b) with the added weight? How would you recommend this be divided up?

2. Can walking efficiency be improved? And if it were, how would that affect caloric balance?

Related Readings

1. Plowman, S.A. & Smith, D.L. (2003). Exercise Physiology for Health, Fitness and Performance (2nd ed.). San Fransisco: Benjamin Cummings.
2. Powers, S.K. & Howley, E.T. (2001). Exercise Physiology: Theory and Application to Fitness and Performance (4th ed.) (pp. 105-107). Boston: McGraw-Hill.
3. McArdle, W.D., Katch, F.I. & Katch, V.L. (2001). Exercise Physiology: Energy, Nutrition and Human Performance (5th ed.) (pp. 197-198, 201-207). Baltimore: Williams & Wilkins.

Caloric Cost and Fuel Utilization

1 Mile Walk Versus 1 Mile Run

Student Learning Objectives

After completing this lab, you should be able to:

1. Define, explain and correctly use key terms.
2. Explain how oxygen consumption (VO_2), respiratory exchange ratio (RER), and energy expenditure are related.
3. Calculate the caloric cost of walking and running the same distance.
4. Explain the interaction between intensity and duration on energy expenditure and fuel utilization.

Equipment

- Motor Driven Treadmill
- O_2 and CO_2 Analyzers
- Noseclip and Mouthpiece

Procedure

The relationship between VO_2, RER and energy expenditure will be examined by comparing the caloric cost of walking and running the same distance. One student whose fitness level will permit walking a mile in 15-20 minutes (4.8-6.4 $km \cdot hr^{-1}$; 3.0 to 4.0 $mi \cdot hr^{-1}$), resting for 5 minutes and then running a mile in 7-10 minutes (9.7-13.8 $km \cdot hr^{-1}$; 8.5 $mi \cdot hr^{-1}$) is selected.

<u>Note to Instructor</u>: This lab can be used to determine the caloric cost of any exercise (cycling, elliptical strider, rowing machine, stairmaster, etc.) if the walk-run comparison is not of interest. However, both bouts of exercise must be in a submaximal, aerobic steady state. That is, RER values need to plateau and be between 0.7 and 0.99.

Protocol

1. Stand quietly for 3 minutes. When gas analysis data indicates relaxation and a true resting state, 3 minutes of resting data are obtained. Gas analysis is continuous from that point.
2. Walk 1 mile at 0% grade at a self-selected pace within the guidelines specified.
3. Sit and rest for 5 minutes.
4. Run 1 mile at 0% grade at a self-selected pace within the guidelines specified.
5. Cool down by walking for 3 minutes.
6. VO_2 and RER are measured and recorded as indicated in Data Table 1.0.

Data Table 1.0

Name:	____________	Age (yr):	____________	Temp (°C):	____________
Training Status:	____________	Ht (cm):	____________	P_B (mmHg):	____________
Sex:	____________	Wt (kg):	____________	RH (%):	____________

Speed ($km \cdot hr^{-1}/mi \cdot hr^{-1}$)	Exercise Time (minutes)	VO_2 ($L \cdot min^{-1}$)	RER	Caloric Equivalent ($kcal \cdot L\ O_2^{-1}$)	Calories ($kcal \cdot min^{-1}$)	%CHO/%FAT
Rest	1					
	2					
	3					
1 Mile Walk	1					
	2					
	3					
	4					
	5					
	6					
	7					
	8					
	9					
	10					
	11					
	12					
	13					
	14					
	15					
	16					
	17					
	18					
	19					
	20					
Mean						

Total Caloric Expenditure for Walk (kcal): ____________ (Do not include resting minutes)

Mean VO_2 ($mL \cdot kg \cdot min^{-1}$):* ____________

Average Caloric Expenditure for Rest ($kcal \cdot min^{-1}$): ____________

* *Note to Student: Convert mean VO_2 $L \cdot min^{-1}$ to VO_2 $mL \cdot min^{-1}$ and then divide by body weight.*

1 Mile Run	1					
	2					
	3					
	4					
	5					
	6					
	7					
	8					
	9					
	10					
	11					
	12					
	13					
	14					
	15					
	16					
	17					
	18					
	19					
	20					
Mean						

Total Caloric Expenditure for Run (kcal): _______________ (Do not include resting minutes)

Mean VO_2 ($mL \cdot kg \cdot min^{-1}$):* _______________

* *Note to Student: Convert mean VO_2 $L \cdot min^{-1}$ to VO_2 $mL \cdot min^{-1}$ and then divide by body weight.*

Student Activities

A. Definitions.

Define the following key terms. For those terms which are measurable variables, describe in your own words what they mean (not how they are obtained or calculated). Indicate the unit(s) of measurement.

1. Caloric Equivalent:

2. Economy:

3. Energy Expenditure:

4. Kilocalorie/Kilojoule:

5. Metabolic Equivalent (MET):

6. Respiratory Exchange Ratio (RER):

B. Analysis

1. Complete data Table 1.0 using a table of caloric equivalents. Calculate both the rate of expenditure ($kcal \cdot min^{-1}$) and total expenditure (kcal) for a) walking 1 mile and b) running 1 mile. Convert these values to kjoules. Compute both gross and net values.

2. Determine the % CHO and % FAT utilized during the 1 mile of walking and 1 mile of running using the average RER value for each mile.

3. Calculate the MET level for walking and running 1 mile.

C. Interpretation and Discussion.

1. Compare and contrast the energy expenditure in kcals/kjoules and METS for walking and running one mile. If you have VO_2 max data, what % VO_2 max does each represent?

2. Compare and contrast the fuel utilization between walking and running one mile.

D. Application.

1. In order to lose 0.5 kg (1.1 lb.) per week by exercise alone, how many miles would the subject in this lab have to a) walk and b) run? Compute using gross and net caloric costs. Is gross or net the better way to measure calories expended during exercise for weight loss? Defend your choice.

2. Provide examples of foods that the subject in this lab could eat to equal the calories expended during the a) 1 mile walk and b) 1 mile run. Give six individual items and serving sizes for the a) 1 mile walk and b) 1 mile run. Do not repeat but come as close to the actual kcal cost as possible for each item.

3. List examples of other physical activities that have comparable MET levels as a) walking 1 mile and b) running 1 mile. Give three specific activities and intensity/duration for a) walking 1 mile and b) running 1 mile. Do not repeat activities.

4. Defend or Refute: The only way to lose body fat is to burn body fat as a fuel.

5. Defend or Refute: Long duration, low intensity exercise is better than moderate duration, moderate to high intensity exercise for weight control.

6. Would you expect these results to be similar or different if a child/adolescent was the subject? That is, are children/adolescents as economical as adults? What practical significance does this have when children/adolescents run or walk with an adult?

Related Readings

1. Plowman, S.A. & Smith, D.L. (2003). Exercise Physiology for Health, Fitness and Performance (2nd ed.). San Fransisco: Benjamin Cummings.
2. Powers, S.K. & Howley, E.T. (2001). Exercise Physiology: Theory and Application to Fitness and Performance (4th ed.) (pp. 103-105). Boston: McGraw-Hill.
3. McArdle, W.D., Katch, F.I. & Katch, V.L. (2001). Exercise Physiology: Energy, Nutrition and Human Performance (5th ed.) (pp. 204-214). Baltimore: Williams & Wilkins.

Body Composition

Criterion and Field Tests

Student Learning Objectives

After completing this lab, you should be able to:

1. Define, explain and correctly use key terms.
2. Describe hydrostatic weighing, skinfolds and bioelectrical impedance (BIA) as methods of assessing body composition.
3. Explain why hydrostatic weighing can be used to estimate body fat and lean body mass.
4. Assess body composition using skinfolds.

Equipment

- Bioelectrical Impedance Unit
- Scale or Strain Gauge
- Skinfold Calipers
- Spirometer or Vitalometer
- Underwater Weighing Tank or Swimming Pool

Procedure

Body composition will be assessed by hydrostatic weighing, skinfolds, BIA and body mass index (BMI) techniques. Prior to lab, select one student to be hydrostatically weighed (HW). This student should come to lab early to have his/her bathing suit weighed (females should wear a two-piece suit). The student should have removed all oils, lotions and or hair care products with soap and water prior to coming to the lab. After the suit is weighed, he/she can change into it. All students will be subjects for the estimation of body composition by the skinfold, BIA and BMI techniques: students should work with a partner and test each other.

Protocols

A. Skinfolds[6]

1. Measure skinfolds on the right side of the body. Pick up the skinfold between the fingertips of the thumb and index finger so that only skin and subcutaneous fat are grabbed. To be sure that the skinfold does not contain any muscle, have the subject contract the underlying muscle and then relax: You should not feel the contraction between your fingers.
2. Apply the calipers about 1 cm from the fingers holding the skinfold at a depth of the double fold, not the groove.
3. Measure the skinfold thickness at each site one time, and repeat the procedure twice for a total of three trials.

Note to Student: Do not take all three measurements at one site and then move to the next site: Always rotate the measurement sites.

4. Compare the measurements and repeat if any differ by more than ± 2 mm.
5. Record your skinfold measurements and those of the designated HW subject in Data Table 1.0.

B. Bioelectrical Impedance Analysis (BIA)

BIA Pre-test Requirments:

- Fast for 5-6 hours, but no more than 12 hours.
- Do not exercise within 8 hours prior to testing.
- Do not consume large amounts of liquid within 4 hours of testing.

- Do not consume caffeine (coffee, tea or cola) or other diuretics within 3 hours of the test.
- Do not consume alcohol within 12 hours of the test.
- Do not void within the last hour prior to testing.
- Do not undergo the analysis if you are ill with the symptoms of a cold or flu.
- Test women 3 days prior to or 7 days following menses for best results.

1. Remove your right shoe and sock.
2. Position yourself on a couch and make sure that your arms are positioned straight along the sides of your body (not contacting the torso), and that your legs are straight and slightly apart (not contacting each other).
3. Your partner will then complete the following steps:

   a. Clean the electrode contact areas using cotton or gauze and alcohol: Rub vigorously to remove grease, oil, dirt and dry skin.
   b. Apply four electrodes: Two on the right foot and two on the right hand.

   - **Electrode 1**
     Placed on the back of the hand just below the joint between the phalanges and metacarpals of the middle and ring fingers.
   - **Electrode 2**
     Placed on the wrist, level with the ulnar head.
   - **Electrode 3**
     Placed on the foot just proximal to the joint between the metatarsals and phalanges of the second and third toe.
   - **Electode 4**
     Placed along a line bisecting the medial and lateral maleoli of the ankle.

   c. Follow the instructions on the BIA unit for obtaining reactance and percent body fat.

4. Record your BIA data and those of the HW subject in Data Table 1.0.

C. Body Mass Index (BMI).

Body mass index is the ratio of body weight (in kilograms) to body height (in meters squared).

Protocol for height measurement:

1. Remove your shoes.
2. If a stadiometer is used, face away from the wall. If a scale is being used, face away from the vertical rod.
3. Stand against the wall with your heels together, and evenly distribute your weight over each foot. Hold your head with the chin level, eyes looking straight ahead and place your hands on hips.
4. Inhale deeply: Your partner records the measurement at the highest point on the head while gently, but firmly, compressing the hair. The measurement is taken to the nearest 0.1 cm or 0.25 in.

> *Note to Student: After recording the height, check to make sure the scale was read correctly.*

5. Record your height and that of the HW subject in Data Table 1.0

Protocol for weight measurement:

1. Remove your shoes.
2. Step onto the center of the scale.
3. Face toward the beam of the scale and evenly distribute your weight over each foot.
4. Your partner stands on the other side of the scale and moves the beam weights until balance is achieved. Weight is recorded to the nearest 0.25 lb. or 0.01 kg.

> *Note to Student: After recording the weight, check to make sure the scale was read correctly.*

5. Return the beam weights to zero.
6. Record your weight and that of the HW subject in Data Table 1.0.

D. Hydrostatic Weighing[1]

1. Obtain the dry land weight of the pre-selected student dressed only in a bathing suit.
2. Measure his/her residual volume or vital capacity and record in Data Table 2.0.
3. Record the tare weight and instruct the subject as follows:[7]
   a. Enter the tank as gently as possible.
   b. Put on the tare weight belt.
   c. Sit back into the underwater weighing chair.
   d. Expel all air while leaning forward, pulling your head to your knees.
   e. Count 1001, 1002, 1003....1010 while holding your breath.
   f. Gently sit up.
4. Record the student's most stable underwater weight during the 10 second breath-hold in Data Table 2.0
5. Repeat steps 3 (d-f) and 4 for a total of 10 trials.

Data Table 1.0

Skinfolds (mm)	**Subject**	**HW Subject**
Triceps (females)	1. ____ 2. ____ M: ____ 3. ____	1. ____ 2. ____ M: ____ 3. ____
Abdomen (males and females)	1. ____ 2. ____ M: ____ 3. ____	1. ____ 2. ____ M: ____ 3. ____
Chest (males)	1. ____ 2. ____ M: ____ 3. ____	1. ____ 2. ____ M: ____ 3. ____
Thigh (males and females)	1. ____ 2. ____ M: ____ 3. ____	1. ____ 2. ____ M: ____ 3. ____
Suprailiac Crest (females)	1. ____ 2. ____ M: ____ 3. ____	1. ____ 2. ____ M: ____ 3. ____
Sum of M Skinfolds		
% Body Fat		
Bioelectrical Impedance (BIA)		
Reactance (ohms)		
% Body Fat		
Body Mass Index (BMI)		
Weight (kg)		
Height (m)		
Weight (kg)/Height (m^2)		

Data Table 2.0

Name: ______________________ Age:______ yr Height:_____ cm Sex: ________

Mass of subject in air (M_A) = weight with suit _______ kg - weight of suit _______ kg = ________ kg

Residual Volume: Complete either A (estimated residual volume) or B (measured residual volume).

A. Estimation of Residual Volume: Subject is seated with nose clip on; subject inhales and exhales maximally 3 times, and on the third breath, the subject bends over and exhales completely. Repeat for three trials. Use highest value to compute residual volume (based on sex) and record in liters.

Vital Capacity (VC): ________ L (1) ________ L (2) ________ L (3) Room Temperature: ________ °C

VC x BTPS factor (Box 1.0): ________ VC x _______ BTPS = ________ L

Estimated Residual Volume for Males:[8]

RV = 0.24 x _______ (VC BTPS) = _______ L (RV)

Estimated Residual Volume for Females:[8]

RV = 0.28 x ______ (VC BTPS) = ______ L (RV)

B. Measured Residual Volume: _______ (L)

Box 1.0 : BTPS Conversion Factors[2]

Temperature (°C)	BTPS Factor
20	1.102
21	1.096
22	1.092
23	1.085
24	1.080
25	1.075
26	1.068
27	1.063
28	1.057
29	1.045
30	1.039

Underwater weighing measures. Use the highest weight if it is obtained more than twice; use the second highest weight if it is obtained more than once. If neither of the first two conditions are met, use the third highest weight obtained.[7]

Trial#: 1. __________ 2. __________ 3. __________ 4. __________ 5. __________

6. __________ 7. __________ 8. __________ 9. __________ 10. __________

Selected Weight (S_W): __________

Water temperature: ________ °C Water density (D_w): __________ Tare weight* (T_w): __________ kg

Mass of subject in water (M_w) = __________ (S_w) - __________ (T_w) = __________ kg

* *Tare weight is the weight of the equipment suspended from the scale without the subject.*

Box 2.0: Estimating Body Density from Skinfold Measurements

Non-Athletic Females

Jackson-Pollack-Ward Generalized Equation for Non-Athletic Females[5]

$D_B = 1.099421 - 0.0009929\ (X_1) + 0.0000023\ (X_1)^2 - 0.0001392\ (X_2)$

Where D_B = body density ($g \cdot cc^{-1}$)

X_1 = sum of triceps, iliac crest and thigh in mm

X_2 = age to nearest year

Athletic Females

Jackson-Pollack-Ward Generalized Equation for Athletic Females[5]

$D_B = 1.0961 - 0.000695\ (X_1) + 0.0000011\ (X_1)^2 - 0.0000714\ (X_2)$

Where D_B = body density ($g \cdot cc^{-1}$)

X_1 = sum of triceps, abdomen, iliac crest and thigh in mm

X_2 = age to nearest year

Athletic and Non-Athletic Males

Jackson-Pollack-Ward Generalized Equation for Athletic and Non-Athletic Males[4]

$D_B = 1.10938 - 0.0008267\ (X_1) + 0.0000016\ (X_1)^2 - 0.0002574\ (X_2)$

Where D_B = body density ($g \cdot cc^{-1}$)

X_1 = sum of chest, abdomen and thigh in mm

X_2 = age to nearest year

Box 3.0: Estimating Body Density Using Hydrostatic Weighing Data

$$\text{Density } (D_B) = \frac{M_A}{[(M_A - M_W)/D_W] - (RV + 0.1)}$$

Where: M_A = mass in air (kg)

M_W = mass in water (kg)

D_W = density of water (based on water temperature)

Example: M_A = 55.2 kg, M_W = 2.1 kg, RV = 1.0126 l, D_W = .9934

$$D_B = \frac{55.2\text{ kg}}{[(55.2\text{ kg} - 2.1\text{ kg})/.9934] - (1.0126\text{ L} + 0.1\text{ L})}$$

$$D_B = \frac{55.2\text{ kg}}{(53.4527\text{ kg}) - (1.1126\text{ L})}$$

$$D_B = \frac{55.2\text{ kg}}{52.3401\text{ L}} = 1.05464\ kg \cdot L^{-1}*$$

$$D_B = 1.05464\ g \cdot cc^{-1}$$

Temperature (°C)	Water Density ($g \cdot cc^{-1}$)
30	.9957
31	.9954
32	.9951
33	.9947
34	.9944
35	.9941
36	.9937
37	.9934
38	.9930
39	.9926
40	.9922

* *Note to Student: In the metric system, 1 L of water (a volume measure) weighs 1 kg (a mass measure) and vice versa. The numerator in this equation represents mass, and the denominator represents volume. Although $kg \cdot L^{-1}$ is an accurate unit, D_B is generally reported in $g \cdot cc^{-1}$ which can be obtained by dividing $kg \cdot L^{-1}$ by 1000. This yields $g \cdot mL^{-1}$. Cubic centimeters (cc) can then be substituted for mL since they are equivalent in the metric system (see Work, Power and Conversions).*

Box 4.0: Calculating Percent Body Fat from Body Density
After calculating body density using either the skinfold equation or the hydrostatic weighing equation, percent body fat can be calculated using the following equation:[1]

$$\% \text{ BF from } D_B = \left[\frac{4.570}{D_B}\right] - 4.142 \times 100$$

For Example: Assuming a D_B of 1.05464,

$$\% \text{ BF} = \left[\frac{4.570}{1.05464}\right] - 4.142 \times 100$$

$$\% \text{ BF} = (4.333 - 4.142) \times 100$$

$$\% \text{ BF} = 0.1913 \times 100$$

$$\% \text{ BF} = 19.13\ \%$$

Box 5.0: Calculating Body Weight at Selected Percent Bodyfat

1. After calculating percent body fat from body density, calculate lean body mass (LBM) using the following equation:

$$\text{LBM (lbs.)} = \text{total weight} \times \left[\frac{100 - \% \text{ BF}}{100}\right]$$

Where total weight is your current body weight in pounds.

2. After calculating LBM, calculate body weight at your selected %BF using the following equation:

$$\text{Body weight at selected \% BF} = \frac{100 \times \text{LBM}}{(100\% - \text{Selected \% BF})}$$

Where selected % BF is based on the following ranges:[3]

Fitness % BF: Males = 12-18%, Females = 16-25%
Athlete's % BF: Males = 5-13%, Females = 12-18%

3. After calculating body weight at your selected % BF, calculate pounds to lose or gain based on your current body weight and the body weight at your selected perecent body fat using the following equation:

current weight - body weight at selected % BF = pounds to lose or gain

For example: A female soccer player who weighs 150 lbs. has a % BF of 25% and wants to be 17% body fat. How much weight must she lose?

1. Calculate LBM: $150 \times \left[\frac{100 - 25}{100}\right] = 112.5$ lbs.

2. Calculate body weight at selected % BF: $\frac{100 \times 112.5 \text{ lbs.}}{100 - 17} = 135.5$ lbs.

3. Calculate the weight difference between current % BF and selected % BF: 150 lbs. - 135.5 lbs. = 14.5 lbs. to lose

Student Actvities

A. Definitions.

Define the following key terms. For those terms which are measurable variables, describe in your own words what they mean (not how they are obtained or calculated). Indicate the unit(s) of measurement.

1. Body Density (D_B):

2. Body Mass Index (BMI):

3. Density:

4. Lean Body Mass (LBM):

5. Percent Body Fat (% BF):

6. Residual Volume (RV):

7. Skinfolds:

B. Analysis.

1. Using skinfold measurements in Data Table 1.0, calculate your % BF and that of HW subject by selecting the appropriate equation for D_B (Box 2.0) and converting D_B to % BF (Box 4.0).

2. Calculate the HW subject's % BF by estimating D_B from the hydrostatic weighing data (Box 3.0) and converting D_B to % BF (Box 4.0).

3. Using skinfolds and BIA, calculate your LBM, body weight at a selected percent and pounds to lose or gain (Box 5.0). If you were the HW subject, calculate LBM, body weight at a selected % BF and pounds to lose or gain using skinfolds, BIA and hydrostatic weighing.

4. If data are available from the *Maximal Oxygen Consumption Field Test: PACER* lab, compute a correlation between % BF calculated using skinfold measurements and estimated VO_2 max from the PACER.

C. Interpretation and Discussion.

1. Compare and contrast your % BF estimated from skinfolds and BIA. Are the values comparable between techniques? Look at the HW subject's % BF calculated from skinfolds, BIA and hydrostatic weighing. Are his/her values comparable between techniques?

2. Discuss how the amount of weight to be gained or lost to reach the weight at your selected % BF varies between techniques (Box 5.0).

3. Females had to select between a non-athletic and an athletic skinfold equation. Why (physiologically)?

4. Discuss the impact of body composition (% BF) on cardiovascular endurance performance.

D. Application.

1. Discuss the advantages and disadvantages of using BMI to assess body composition in a school setting.

2. How should advice regarding weight to gain or lose be modified based on the technique used to determine % BF? Describe and consider the error of measurement for each technique.

References

1. Brozek, J., Grande, F., Anderson, J.T. & Keys, A. (1963). Densitometric analysis of body composition: revision of some quantitative assumptions. New York Academy of Sciences, 110, 113-140.
2. Consolazio, C.F., Johnson, R.E. & Pecora, I.J. (1963). Physiologic Measurements of Metabolic Functions in Man. New York: McGraw-Hill Book Co.
3. Doxey, G.E., Fairbanks, B., Housh, T.H., Johnson, G.O., Datch, F. & Lohman, T.G. (1987). Body Composition Roundtable: Table 1. Scientific Considerations. National Strength and Conditioning Association Journal, 9, 14-15.
4. Jackson, A.S. & Pollock, M.L. (1978). Generalized equations for predicting body density of men. British Journal of Nutrition, 40, 497-504.
5. Jackson, A.S., Pollock, M.L. & Ward, A. (1980). Generalized equations for predicting body density of women. Medicine and Science in Sport and Exercise, 92, 175-182.
6. Lohman, T.G., Roche, A.F. & Martorell, R. (eds.) (1988). Anthropometric Standardization Reference Manual. Champaign, IL: Human Kinetics.
7. Sinning, W. (1975). Experiments and Demonstrations in Exercise Physiology (pp. 41-53). Philadelphia: W. B. Saunders Co.
8. Wilmore, J.H. (1969). The use of actual, predicted and constant residual volumes in the assessment of body composition by underwater weighing. Medicine and Science in Sport and Exercise, 1, 87-90.

Related Readings

1. Plowman, S.A. & Smith, D.L. (2003). Exercise Physiology for Health, Fitness and Performance (2nd ed.). San Fransisco: Benjamin Cummings.
2. Powers, S.K. & Howley, E.T. (2001). Exercise Physiology: Theory and Application to Fitness and Performance (4th ed.) (pp. 344-351). Boston: McGraw-Hill.
3. McArdle, W.D., Katch, F.I. & Katch, V.L.(2001). Exercise Physiology: Energy, Nutrition and Human Performance (5th ed.) (pp. 766-778). Baltimore: Williams & Wilkins.

The Influence of Carbohydrate Replacement on Fuel Utilization

To Supplement or Not?

Student Learning Objectives

After completing this lab, you should be able to:

1. Define, explain and correctly use key terms.
2. Compare and contrast the effects of carbohydrate replacement versus water replacement on exercise performance.

Equipment

- Heart Rate Watches/Transmitter Straps
- Lactate Analyzer and Accessories
- Motordriven Treadmill or Cycle Ergometer
- O_2 and CO_2 Analyzers
- Pneumoscan Flow Meter or Pneumotach
- Sphygmomanometer/Cuff/Stethoscope
- Sports Drink (6-8% CHO concentration)

Procedure

The effects of carbohydrate replacement on exercise performance will be examined by performing 60-90 minutes of aerobic exercise under two different conditions: water consumption and carbohydrate "sports drink" consumption. Determine which students will be subjects. Suggestions:

- The same student or all students perform both protocols, in which case at least 24 hours should separate exercise days.
- A different student or half of the class performs one of the protocols.
- One male and one female of equal training status perform both protocols.
- Two or three students of the same sex but different training status (non-exerciser, aerobically trained, resistance trained) each perform both protocols.

If students are completing both protocols, at least 24 hours should separate test days, and care should be

taken to administer the exercise tests under similar conditions (i.e., same or similar clothing, time of day, etc.). Use the 24 hour inventory in *Appendix C* to check this. If students do both tests, randomize the order.

Pre-Exercise Conditions:

- Do not eat 4-12 hours prior to testing. Be consistent for both tests.
- Water intake is encouraged. However, avoid alcohol, coffee, tea, fruit juices, soda, electrolyte drinks, etc.

Protocols

> *Note to Student: The mouthpiece used for gas analysis will have to be removed and the metabolic analysis placed on "pause" while the subject drinks. It may take some time to re-stabilize the O_2 and CO_2 values once the subject resumes breathing through the mouthpiece. Make sure you know which minutes to exclude and which to include for analysis.*

Select and prepare exercise equipment.

A. Water Replacement

1. Consume 200 ml of water prior to exercise.
2. Select a workrate that will elicit a heart rate of

135-140 b·min^{-1} within the first 5 minutes of exercise, or utilize the same workrate from the carbohydrate "sports drink" replacement trial.

3. Record workrate in Data Table 1.0.
4. Sustain workrate for 50 to 120 minutes, consuming 200 ml of water every 15 minutes during exercise.
5. Heart rate (HR), blood pressure (BP), oxygen consumption (VO_2) and respiratory exchange ratio (RER) are measured and recorded as indicated in Data Table 1.0.

B. Carbohydrate "Sports Drink" Replacement

1. Select a workrate that will elicit a heart rate of 135-140 b·min^{-1} within the first 5 minutes of exercise, or utilize same workrate from the water replacement trial.
2. Record workrate in Data Table 2.0.
3. Consume 200 ml of a "sports drink" (6-8% [CHO]) prior to exercise.
4. Sustain workrate for 50 to 120 minutes, consuming 200 ml of a "sports drink" (6-8% [CHO]) every 15 minutes during exercise.
5. HR, BP, VO_2 and RER are measured and recorded as indicated in Data Table 2.0.

Data Table 1.0: Water Replacement

Name: ____________		Age (yr): ________		Temp (°C): ________	
Training Status: ____________		Ht (cm): ________		P_B (mmHg): ________	
Sex: ____________		Wt (kg): ________		RH (%): ________	
Workrate: ____________		(@ 135-140 b·min^{-1})		Circle:	T_1 T_2

Time (minutes)	HR (b·min^{-1})	BP (mmHg)	RPE	VO_2 (mL·kg^{-1}·min^{-1})	RER
Rest					
5					
10					
15					
20					
25					
30					
35					
40					
45					
50					
55					
60					
65					
70					
75					
80					
85					
90					
95					
100					
105					
110					
115					
120					

Data Table 2.0: Carbohydrate Replacement

Name: ____________________ Age (yr): __________ Temp (°C): __________

Training Status: ____________________ Ht (cm): __________ P_B (mmHg): __________

Sex: ____________________ Wt (kg): __________ RH (%): __________

Workrate: ____________________ (@ 135-140 b·min^{-1}) Circle: T_1 T_2

Time (minutes)	HR (b·min^{-1})	BP (mmHg)	RPE	VO_2 (mL·kg^{-1}·min^{-1})	RER
Rest					
5					
10					
15					
20					
25					
30					
35					
40					
45					
50					
55					
60					
65					
70					
75					
80					
85					
90					
95					
100					
105					
110					
115					
120					

Student Activities

A. Definitions.

Define the following key terms. For those terms which are measurable variables, describe in your own words what they mean (not how they are obtained or calculated). Indicate the unit(s) of measurement.

1. Carbohydrate (CHO):

2. Energy Expenditure:

3. Fuel Utilization:

4. Metabolic Mixture:

B. Analysis.

1. Graph the VO_2 response to exercise with and without carbohydrate replacement. Place VO_2 on the Y-axis and time on the X-axis. This should be a line graph.
2. Graph the RER response to exercise with and without carbohydrate replacement. Place RER on the Y-axis and time on the X-axis. This should be a line graph.
3. Graph the RPE response to exercise with and without carbohydrate replacement. Place RPE on the Y-axis and time on the X-axis. This should be a lie graph.

C. Interpretation and Discussion.

1. Discuss the VO_2 and RER responses to exercise with and without carbohydrate replacement. What does the data say about energy expenditure and fuel utilization during moderate, long duration exercise?

2. Discuss the RPE responses to exercise with and without carbohydrate replacement.

3. Were any physiological differences observed between the two conditions? If so, what? What is/are the physiological explanation(s) which account for the differences observed during exercise with and without carbohydrate replacement?

D. Application.

1. How is carbohydrate ingestion related to maintaining exercise intensity during:
   a. a century (100 mile) bicycle race
   b. a highschool soccer game (80 minutes: Not a goal keeper)
   c. a pole vault or high jump competition (≤ 8 jumps)
   d. Wimbleton All England Grass Court Championships
   e. the finalists in the State Wrestling Championship

Related Readings

1. Plowman, S.A. & Smith, D.L. (2003). Exercise Physiology for Health, Fitness and Performance (2nd ed.). San Fransisco: Benjamin Cummings.
2. Powers, S.K. & Howley, E.T. (2001). Exercise Physiology: Theory and Application to Fitness and Performance (4th ed.) (pp. 438-442). Boston: McGraw-Hill.
3. McArdle, W.D., Katch, F.I. & Katch, V.L.(2001). Exercise Physiology: Energy, Nutrition and Human Performance (5th ed.) (pp. 92-101). Baltimore: Williams & Wilkins.

Hyperventilation and Breath Holding

Control of Pulmonary Ventilation

Student Learning Objectives

After completing this lab, you should be able to:

1. Define, explain and correctly use key terms.
2. Describe the effects of hyperventilation, carbon dioxide (CO_2) re-breathing and exercise on breath-hold time.
3. Describe the effects of hyperventilation and hypoventilation on arterial partial pressure of CO_2 ($PaCO_2$) and arterial partial pressure of oxygen (PaO_2).

Equipment

- Metronome
- Plastic Bags/Paper Sacks
- Stopwatches

Procedure

The effects of hyperventilation, CO_2 re-breathing and exercise on breath-hold time will be examined. All students will be subjects.

Note to Student: If you have a tendency to faint, please notify the laboratory instructor — it may be best if you simply observe. If you participate and feel faint or dizzy, stop immediately and re-breathe your expired air by cupping your hands over your nose and mouth for a few minutes.

Protocols

Note to Instructor: You may wish to prepare an audiotape to synchronize and standardize the timing of the ventilation sequences. Students may compare their own data (Data Table 1.0) among protocols, or a statistical analysis of mean data (Data Table 2.0) may be conducted.

A. Normal Breathing: Baseline

1. Following normal tidal breathing, inhale and begin a breath-hold.
2. Time the length of the breath-hold and record in Data Table 1.0.
3. Rest for 2 minutes.

B. 30 Second Hyperventilation

1. With a metronome set to 40 beats·min^{-1}, complete one respiratory cycle (inhalation and exhalation) per 3 seconds for 30 seconds, inhaling and exhaling as deeply as possible.
2. At the end of 30 seconds (the 11th inspiration) begin a breath-hold.
3. Time the length of the breath-hold and record in Data Table 1.0.
4. Rest for 2 minutes.

C. 90 Second Bag Breathing

1. Breathe in and out of a bag held snugly around your mouth and nose for 90 seconds.

Note to Student: Breathe normally during this experiment — do not hyperventilate.

2. At the end of 90 seconds, inhale the air from the bag and begin a breath-hold.
3. Time the length of the breath-hold and record in

Data Table 1.0.

4. Rest for 2 minutes.

D. 90 Second Hyperventilation

1. With a metronome set to 40 beats·min^{-1}, complete one respiratory cycle (inhalation and exhalation) per 3 seconds for 90 seconds, inhaling and exhaling as deeply as possible.
2. At the end of 90 seconds, begin a breath-hold.
3. Time the length of the breath-hold and record in Data Table 1.0.
4. Rest for 2 minutes.

E. 2 Minute Run in Place

1. With a metronome set to 176 beats·min^{-1}, run in place for two minutes.
2. At the end of the run, take one deep breath, exhale, inhale and begin a breath-hold.
3. Time the length of the breath-hold and record in Data Table 1.0.
4. Rest for 2 minutes.

Data Table 1.0 Breath-Hold Time (Seconds)				
Normal Breathing: Baseline	30 Second Hyperventiltion	90 Second Bag Breathing	90 Second Hyperventilation	2 Minute Run in Place
_______ (s)	_______ (s)	_______ (s)	_______ (s)	_______ (s)

Data Table 2.0 Breath-Hold Time (Seconds)					
Subject	Normal Breathing: Baseline	30 Second Hyperventilation	90 Second Bag Breathing	90 Second Hyperventilation	2 Minute Run in Place
1					
2					
3					
4					
5					
6					
7					
8					
9					
10					
11					
12					
13					
14					
15					
16					
17					
18					
19					
20					
Mean					
SD					

Student Activities

A. Definitions.

Define the following key terms. For those terms which are measurable variables, describe in your own words what they mean (not how they are obtained or calculated). Indicate the unit(s) of measurement.

1. Hypercapnia:

2. Hyperventilation:

3. Hypocapnia:

4. Hypoventilation:

5. Arterial Partial Pressure of Carbon Dioxide ($PaCO_2$):

6. Arterial Partial Pressure of Oxygen (PaO_2):

7. Pulmonary Ventilation:

B. Analysis.

1. Using the class data in Data Table 2.0, create a bar graph using the mean time for each of the 5 breathing conditions.

C. Interpretation and Discussion.

1. For each of the 4 experimental breathing conditions, indicate whether hypocapnia or hypercapnia should have occurred, theoretically.

2. Based on your results, determine whether hypercapnia or hypocapnia actually occurred for each activity; that is, determine and report if there is a significant difference between the mean time for the Normal Breathing: Baseline breath-hold and the mean time for a) 30 Second Hyperventilation, b) 90 Second Bag Breathing, c) 90 Second Hyperventilation and d) 2 Minute Run in Place.

3. What happens to PaO_2 mmHg as a result of hyperventilation?

4. What happens to $PaCO_2$ mmHg as a result of hyperventilation?

5. Compare and contrast the role of hypoxia with hypercapnia as stimulators of ventilation.

D. Application.

1. What are the advantages and disadvantages of hyperventilating?

Related Readings

1. Plowman, S.A. & Smith, D.L. (2003). Exercise Physiology for Health, Fitness and Performance (2nd ed.). San Fransisco: Benjamin Cummings.
2. Powers, S.K. & Howley, E.T. (2001). Exercise Physiology: Theory and Application to Fitness and Performance (4th ed.) (pp. 202-207). Boston: McGraw-Hill.
3. McArdle, W.D., Katch, F.I. & Katch, V.L. (2001). Exercise Physiology: Energy, Nutrition and Human Performance (5th ed.) (pp. 286-290). Baltimore: Williams & Wilkins.

Static and Dynamic Lung **Volumes**

Creating a Spirogram

Student Learning Objectives

After completing this lab, you should be able to:

1. Define, explain and correctly use key terms.
2. Measure and analyze static lung volumes and capacities.
3. Measure and analyze dynamic lung volumes (air flow rates).
4. Describe the difference between static and dynamic in relation to lung volumes.

Equipment

- Mouthpieces/Noseclips
- Wet or Dry Spirometer (if possible with capacity for gas dilution) and compatible computer (with designated respiratory software) or recording chart paper and pens

Procedure

Static lung volumes and capacities and dynamic lung volumes will be measured. As many students as possible should be subjects. Alternately, determine which students will be subjects. Suggestions:

- One or all students perform all four protocols.
- Land aerobic endurance trained individual, male or female, and water aerobic endurance trained individual, male or female.
- Aerobic endurance trained individual, male or female, and dynamic resistance trained individual, male or female.
- One male and one female whose activity lifestyle (sedentary or trained in same modality) is similar.

Protocols

<u>Note</u>: Make sure all equipment has been properly sanitized and that mouthpieces are not handled prior to testing. Students with upper respiratory infections (colds) should be omitted from testing. Subjects should not have exercised for at least 30 minutes prior to testing since prior activity may decrease some variables, such as vital capacity, and increase others, such as residual volume. No significant differences occur between values obtained when the subject is sitting or standing. However, if normative comparisons are desired, the posture should match that of the original data collection.

Prior to any testing, each test should be explained and the required breathing pattern demonstrated using the spirometer. The subject should practice before actual data collection and should be encouraged during actual data collection.

A. <u>Slow Vital Capacity (SVC)</u>

The determination of vital capacity (VC) actually measures inspiratory reserve volume (IRV), tidal volume (V_T) and expiratory reserve volume (ERV), since VC = IRV + V_T + ERV. Speed of exhalation during the SVC test is not a priority.

1. Place a noseclip on your nose and ascertain that you cannot breathe through the nose.
2. Place your mouth tightly around the mouthpiece.
3. Breathe normally until your tidal volume is

relaxed and uniform.

4. When instructed to do so, inspire maximally and expire maximally.
5. Return to normal (tidal) breathing.
6. Record data in Data Table 1.0.

B. Forced Vital Capacity (FVC)

The difference between performing a SVC test and a forced vital capacity (FVC) test is, as the name implies, the the speed of exhalation. The variables determined from this test include FVC, forced expiratory volume in 1 and 3 seconds (FEV_1 & FEV_3) and the percentage of FVC expired in 1 second (FEV_1/FVC).

1. Place a noseclip on your nose and ascertain that you cannot breathe through the nose.
2. Place your mouth tightly around the mouthpiece.
3. Breathe normally until your tidal volume is relaxed and uniform.
4. When instructed to do so, inspire maximally, expire maximally (both in terms of speed and force) and inspire maximally again.
5. Return to normal (tidal) breathing.
6. Record data in Data Table 1.0.

C. Maximal Voluntary Ventilation (MVV)

This test measures only one variable, the maximal amount of air an individual is able to ventilate pro-rated to one minute.

1. Place a noseclip on your nose and ascertain that you cannot breathe through the nose.
2. Place your mouth tightly around the mouthpiece.
3. Breathe normally until your tidal volume is relaxed and uniform.
4. When instructed to do so, perform fast maximal inspirations and expirations for 12 or 15 seconds.
5. Return to normal (tidal) breathing.
6. Record data in Data Table 1.0.

D. Residual Volume (RV)

Residual volume is most frequently determined by a technique called gas dilution. The two primary options are helium dilution and nitrogen washout. In the first technique, a known amount of helium is mixed with the unknown amount of air in the lungs. The concentration of helium decreases in proportion to that of the unknown volume. In the nitrogen washout technique, the dilution of medical grade oxygen and changes in nitrogen concentration are measured.

1. Place a noseclip on your nose and ascertain that you cannot breathe through the nose.
2. Place your mouth tightly around the mouthpiece.
3. Breathe normally until your tidal volume is relaxed and uniform.
4. Follow the instructions for the technique and equipment being used.
5. Return to normal (tidal) breathing.
6. Record data in Data Table 1.0.

If RV cannot be measured directly from one of the gas dilution techniques, it may be estimated from the SVC. If you have a SVC (BTPS) value, RV can be estimated using one of the following equations:[3]

Males:

= 0.24 x corrected VC (BTPS)
= 0.24 x _______ (L)
= _______ (L)

Females:

= 0.28 x corrected VC (BTPS)
= 0.28 x _______ (L)
= _______ (L)

Note to Student: See the Body Composition lab for calculation of corrected SVC from ATPS to BTPS.

Indicate the technique used to obtain the RV: ____________________________________

Data Table 1.0*			
	Subject #1	Subject #2	Subject #3
Subject Description			
Age			
Sex			
Height (cm)			
Weight (kg)			
Activity History			
Respiratory Variables			
SVC (L)			
IC (L)			
ERV (L)			
TV (L)			
TLC (L)			
FRC (L)			
RV (L)			
RV/TLC (%)			
FVC (L)			
FVC_1 (L)			
FVC_1/FVC (%)			
TV/VC (%)			
MVV ($L \cdot min^{-1}$)			

* *<u>Note to Instructor</u>: Rows are left blank for any additional variables you may ask the students to evaluate.*

Student Activities

A. Definitions.

Define the following key terms. For those terms which are measurable variables, describe in your own words what they mean (not how they are obtained or calculated). Indicate the unit(s) of measurement.

1. Forced Vital capacity (FVC):

2. Maximal Voluntary Ventilation (MVV):

3. Residual Volume (RV):

4. Slow Vital Capacity (SVC):

5. Spirometry:

6. Tidal Volume (V_T):

7. Total Lung Capacity (TLC):

B. Analysis.

1. Complete Data Table 1.0 from the computer print-outs or spirometer tracings. In some cases, a calculation from available data may be necessary. Attach the computer print-outs or spirometer tracings when you hand this table in.

2. Using your personal data, or the subject closest to you in description, prepare a spirogram of the four static volumes and four static capacities. Use your SVC not FVC value. Spirogram figures from Plowman and Smith[2] or other Exercise Physiology textbooks may be used as a guideline, but you must include actual values properly proportioned.

C. Interpretation and Discussion.

1. Compare and contrast the actual versus predicted values for the subject whose spirogram you presented. Include all variables in your discussion for which you have predicted values not just those used in the spirogram. Use the predicted values from your computer print-out or, if you do not have a computer print-out, those presented in Box 1.0 below and/or other sources. What do these results mean? That is, were they good or bad differences? What might explain any differences from the predicted values?

Box 1.0		
Approximate Lung Volumes and Capacities in mL for Healthy, Seated, Young Adults (20-30yr)[1]		
Volume/Capacity	Males	Females
Inspiratory Reserve Volume	3100	1900
Tidal Volume (V_T)	400-600	350-500
Expiratory Reserve Volume (ERV)	1200	800
Residual Volume (RV)	1200	1000
Inspiratory Capacity (IC)	3600	2400
Functional Residual Capacity (FRC)	2400	1800
Vital Capacity (VC)	4800	3200
Total Lung Capacity (TLC)	6000	4200

2. Theoretically compare the expected values for either land versus water trained individuals or aerobic endurance versus dynamic resistance trained individuals. If you have data, compare and contrast the results of your subject with the expected results.

D. Application

1. What practical implications do the comparative results (Section B, #2) have?

2. Which of the respiratory variables, if any, can be used as predictors or measures of physical fitness or athletic potential?

3. Which of the respiratory variables in Box 1.0, if any, can be used as predictors of health status?

References

1. Comroe, J.H., Forster, R.E., Dubois, A.B., Briscose, W.A. & Carlsen, E. (1962). The Lung (2nd ed.). Chicago: Year Book Medical Publishers.
2. Plowman, S.A. & Smith, D.L. (2003). Exercise Physiology for Health, Fitness and Performance. San Francisco: Benjamin Cummings.
3. Wilmore, J.H. (1969). The use of actual, predicted and constant residual volumes in the assessment of body composition by underwater weighing. Medicine and Science in Sport and Exercise, 1, 87-90.

Related Readings

1. Plowman, S.A. & Smith, D.L. (2003). Exercise Physiology for Health, Fitness and Performance (2nd ed.). San Francisco: Benjamin Cummings.
2. Powers, S.K. & Howley, E.T. (2001). Exercise Physiology: Theory and Application to Fitness and Performance (4th ed.) (pp. 191-192). Boston: McGraw-Hill.
3. McArdle, W.D., Katch, F.I. & Katch, V.L. (2001). Exercise Physiology: Energy, Nutrition and Human Performance (5th ed.) (pp. 257-261). Baltimore: Williams & Wilkins. pp.

Heart Rate and Blood Pressure

Acute Responses to Aerobic and Resistance Exercise

Student Learning Objectives

After completing this lab, you should be able to:

1. Define, explain and correctly use key terms.
2. Measure blood pressure and heart rate (HR) at rest, during exercise and recovery.
3. Calculate pulse pressure (PP), mean arterial pressure (MAP) and rate pressure product (RPP) at rest, during exercise and recovery.
4. Describe the difference in the blood pressure response between aerobic and resistance exercise.

Equipment

- Blood Pressure Cuff
- Cycle Ergometer
- Dumbbells
- Heart Rate Watches/Transmitter Straps
- Sphygmomanometer
- Stethoscopes (single and double)
- Stopwatches
- Tape Measure

Procedure

Heart rate and blood pressure will be measured at rest and during aerobic and resistance exercise. All students will practice measuring HR and blood pressure described in Protocols A, B and C; work with a partner and test each other. Two students should be selected to be subjects for determining the HR and blood pressure responses to aerobic and resistance exercise (Protocols D and E).

Protocols

A. Heart Rate Determination

1. Feel for your partner's pulse at the radial and carotid arteries. Use the tips of the index and middle fingers—do not use the thumb. When palpating the carotid artery, press lightly: Too much pressure stimulates the vagus nerve which causes the HR to decrease. This method of determining HR is called *palpation*.
2. Listen to your partner's heart beat with a stethoscope. Usually, the best sound is heard by positioning the stethoscope over the apex of the heart. This method of determining HR is called *auscultation*.
3. Measure your partner's HR using each of the 2 methods described above.
4. Start the stopwatch when the heart beat is felt or heard and count the first beat as zero.
5. Continue counting beats for the time specified in Data Table 1.0: Always convert to beats per minute ($b \cdot min^{-1}$).
6. Record HR in Data Table 1.0.

Data Table 1.0

Measurement Site	Counted Beats	Convert to $b \cdot min^{-1}$	HR $b \cdot min^{-1}$
Radial Pulse (1 min)		x 1	
Carotid Pulse (15 s)		x 4	
Auscultation (6 s)		x 10	
Your Choice (10 s)		x 6	

B. Blood Pressure[1]

1. Your partner should be seated with his/her arm and back properly supported with his/her feet flat on the floor (legs should not be crossed).
2. Remove restrictive clothing from the arm to be used for measurement and position the arm at heart level.
3. Determine the appropriate cuff size (if using velcro cuffs) according to the following chart:

Relaxed Biceps Circumference	Size of Cuff
33-47 cm	Large Adult
25-35 cm	Adult
18-26 cm	Child

4. Place the appropriate cuff on the arm approximately 1 inch (2.54 cm) above the antecubital space with the center of the air bladder over the brachial artery; the brachial artery can be located by slightly hyperextending the elbow and palpating the medial portion of the space.
5. Adjust the sphygmomanometer so that it is at eye level.
6. Place the stethoscope over the brachial artery and inflate the cuff to one of the following levels:

- 160 mmHg
- 20 mmHg above the subject's expected or known blood pressure
- 30 mmHg above the disappearance of the subject's radial pulse

7. Adjust the air release screw so that the mercury falls approximately 3 mmHg per heartbeat or 3 mmHg per second.
8. Listen for the following sounds (*Korotkoff* sounds: Box 1.0):

1st Sound
- Sharp tap or thud caused by sudden vibration due to the rush of blood (systolic blood pressure: SBP).

2nd Sound
- Metallic tapping sound; may be softer than 1st sound.

3rd Sound
- Continuous thudding.

4th Sound
- Muffling, softened flowing sound (diastolic blood pressure-one: DBP_1).

5th Sound
- Last sound, followed by total silence (diastolic blood pressure-two: DBP_2); usually 7 to 10 mmHg lower than DBP_1.

Box 1.0
Korotkoff Sounds

	Sounds	
		120 mmHg
I	Onset of sharp, rythmical thuds.	
II	Whooshing sounds or soft metallic tapping.	There can be considerable inter-individual variation in sounds II and III
III	Soft rythmical thuds.	
		86 mmHg
IV	Noticeable drop in volume: Muffling or tone change.	
		80 mmHg
V	Silence.	

SBP: Onset of sharp, rythmical thuds (I)
DBP_1: Noticeable drop in volume: Tone change (IV)
DBP_2: Last sound heard before silence (V)

9. Rapidly deflate the cuff after obtaining the blood pressure readings—it is painful for your partner to maintain a partial constriction of the blood vessel.
10. Measure and record blood pressure at least 3 times or until you feel you have obtained an accurate reading.

Note to Student: Have your instructor check your accuracy by listening through a double stethoscope.

11. Record blood pressures in Data Table 2.0.

For recording blood pressures, the American Heart Association recommends the following:

- Initially, blood pressure is taken in both arms. If the pressure differs by more than 10 mmHg between the right and left arm, use the arm with the higher pressure. Otherwise, ease of measurement may dictate the use of the right or left arm.
- For resting blood pressure, at least two readings are taken, and there should be a minimum of 1 minute between readings.
- Use DBP_1 for children always.
- Use DBP_1 for adults if sounds are heard at rest below 40 mmHg.
- Use DBP_1 during exercise.
- Use DBP_2 for adults at rest if no sounds are heard below 40 mmHg.
- Always record and state the blood pressure as $SBP/DBP_1/DBP_2$ mmHg.

Data Table 2.0

SBP (mmHg)	DBP_1 (mmHg)	DBP_2 (mmHg)

C. Concurrent Determination of Heart Rate and Blood Pressure

1. Determine your partner's SBP, close the air screw to stop the mercury from dropping, and count the number of beats in 6 seconds.
2. Open the air screw and determine DBP_1 and DBP_2.
3. Record HR (# of beats in 6 seconds x 10) and blood pressure in Data Table 3.0.

Data Table 3.0

SBP (mmHg)	DBP_1 (mmHg)	DBP_2 (mmHg)	HR ($b \cdot min^{-1}$)

D. Cycle Ergometer Ride

1. Wear a HR monitor for comparison to check manual HR count.

Note to Student: The HR column in Data Table 4.0, 5.0 and 6.0 have a column for a) manual HR measurement and b) HR measured using a monitor.

2. Females should work at a rate of 0.5 to 1 kp (150 to 300 $kgm \cdot min^{-1}$) at 50 $rev \cdot min^{-1}$ for 15 minutes. Males should work at 1.5 to 2 kp (450 to 600 $kgm \cdot min^{-1}$) at 50 $rev \cdot min^{-1}$ for 15 minutes.
3. HR and blood pressure (SBP/DBP) are measured at rest, every third minute during exercise and after 1 minute of post-exercise recovery and recorded in Data Table 4.0.

Note: Make sure you do not grip the handlebars while the blood pressure is being measured.

Data Table 4.0

Time (minutes)	SBP (mmHg)	DBP_1 (mmHg)	DBP_2 (mmHg)	HR ($b \cdot min^{-1}$)	
				a	b
Rest					
3					
6					
9					
12					
15					
1 Min Post					

E. Constant Load Resistance Exercise

1. Wear a HR monitor for comparison to check manual HR count.
2. Sit with your left arm free to do a one-arm biceps curl (or any other resistance exercise that is convenient).
3. Choose a weight that you can lift about 15 times for one set.

4. Lift at a cadence of 2 seconds to lift the weight and 2 seconds to lower the weight.

> Note: *Make sure you exhale while lifting the weight and inhale while lowering the weight.*

5. Complete 5 sets of 15 repetitions using the same load, resting 1 minute between each set.
6. HR, SBP and DBP are measured at rest, during the last 20 seconds of each set and after 1 minute of post-exercise recovery and recorded in Data Table 5.0.

Data Table 5.0
Constant Load

Set	Weight	SBP (mmHg)	DBP_1 (mmHg)	DBP_2 (mmHg)	HR ($b \cdot min^{-1}$)	
					a	b
Rest						
1						
2						
3						
4						
5						
1 Minute Post						

E. Incremental Resistance Exercise

1. Wear a HR monitor for comparison to check manual heart rate count.
2. Sit with your left arm free to do a one-arm biceps curl (or other resistance exercise that is convenient). The same exercise from Protocol D should be used.
3. Choose a light weight for set 1 and use a heavier weight each succeeding set.
4. Lift at a cadence of 2 seconds to lift the weight and 2 seconds to lower the weight.

> Note: *Make sure you exhale while lifting the weight and inhale while lowering the weight.*

5. Complete 5 sets, lifting for 1 minute and resting 1 minute between sets.
6. HR, SBP and DBP are measured at rest, during the last 20 seconds of each set and after 1 minute of post-exercise recovery and recorded in Data Table 6.0.

Data Table 6.0
Incremental Load

Set	Weight	SBP (mmHg)	DBP_1 (mmHg)	DBP_2 (mmHg)	HR ($b \cdot min^{-1}$)	
					a	b
Rest						
1						
2						
3						
4						
5						
1 Minute Post						

Student Activities

A. Definitions.

Define the following key terms. For those terms which are measurable variables, describe in your own words what they mean (not how they are obtained or calculated). Indicate the unit(s) of measurement.

1. Diastolic Blood Pressure (DBP):

2. Diastolic Blood Pressure-One (DBP_1):

3. Diastolic Blood Pressure-Two (DBP_2):

4. Mean Arterial Pressure (MAP):

5. Rate Pressure Product (RPP):

6. Systolic Blood Pressure (SBP):

B. Analysis.

1. Calculate the following variables for the cycle ergometer ride, constant load resistance exercise and incremental resistance exercise:

   a. Pulse Pressure:
      $PP = SBP - DBP_1$ (exercise) or DBP_2 (rest/recovery)
   b. Mean Arterial Pressure (rest/recovery):
      $MAP = 1/3\ PP + DBP_2$
   c. Mean Arterial Pressure (exercise):
      $MAP = 1/2\ PP + DBP_1$
   d. Rate Pressure Product:
      $RPP = [SBP \times HR] \div 100$

Note to Student: There is no unit of measurement for the variable RPP. Which DBP you use depends on whether the blood pressure was taken during rest, exercise or recovery.

For example: A student rode a cycle ergometer for 15 minutes at a moderate intensity. His blood pressure and HR at rest were 118/86/78 mmHg and 74 b·min^{-1}, respectively, and his blood pressure and HR at minute 15 were 136/90/80 mmHg and 150 b·min^{-1}, respectively.

At rest:
PP = 118 - 78 = 40 mmHg
MAP = [40/3] + 78 = 91.3 mmHg
RPP = [118 x 74] ÷ 100 = 87.32

During exercise:
PP = 136 - 90 = 46 mmHg
MAP = [46/2] + 90 = 113 mmHg
RPP = [136 x 150] ÷ 100 = 204

2. If the *Maximal Oxygen Consumption* lab has been completed, calculate RPP for the incremental portion of the VO_2 max test.

3. Graph the subject's blood pressure response (SBP, DBP_1 and/or DBP_2, and MAP) to the 15 minute cycle ergometer ride (rest, exercise at designated minutes and 1 minute post-exercise).

4. Graph the subject's blood pressure response (SBP, DBP_1 and/or DBP_2, and MAP) to the constant load resistance exercise and the incremental resistance exercise (rest, exercise by set/weight and 1 minute post-exercise).

5. Graph the subject's HR response to the 15 minute cycle ergometer ride (rest, exercise at designated minutes and 1 minute post-exercise).

6. Graph the subject's HR response to the constant load resistance exercise and the incremental resistance exercise (rest, exercise by set/weight and 1 minute post-exercise).

7. Graph the subject's RPP response to the 15 minute cycle ergometer ride, constant load resistance exercise and incremental resistance exercise (rest, exercise at designated minutes or by set/weight and 1 minute post-exercise).

C. Interpretation and Discussion.

1. On the basis of all your graphs, compare and contrast the patterns of cardiovascular responses a) between incremental aerobic exercise based on the *Maximal Oxygen Consumptionm* lab, your textbook and the incremental resistance exercise performed in this lab and b) between steady state submaximal aerobic exercise and constant load resistance exercise.

2. Explain what RPP means (indicates) physiologically.

3. Why does DBP respond differently to a continuous aerobic activity compared to a static or dynamic resistance activity?

D. Application.

1. How may RPP be used in a practical situation?

2. Among the instructions given for taking blood pressure during the cycle ergometer ride was the caution not to grip the handlebars when the blood pressure measurement was being taken. What is the physiological reason for this caution, and how would you expect the values you graphed to change if the handlebars were gripped tightly?

3. Among the instructions given for taking blood pressure during the resistance exercise was the caution to make sure that the subject was not holding his/her breath but instead was exhaling as the weight was lifted and inhaling as the weight was lowered. What is the physiological reason for this caution, and how would you expect the values you graphed to change if the subject was holding his/her breath?

Reference

1. American Society of Hypertension Public Policy Position Paper (1992). Recommendations for Routine Blood Pressure Measurement by Indirect Cuff Sphygmomanometry. American Journal of Hypertension, 5, 207-209.

Related Readings

1. Plowman, S.A. & Smith, D.L. (2003). Exercise Physiology for Health, Fitness and Performance (2nd ed.). San Francisco: Benjamin Cummings.
2. Powers, S.K. & Howley, E.T. (2001). Exercise Physiology: Theory and Application to Fitness and Performance (4th ed.) (pp. 161-163, 176-180). Boston: McGraw-Hill.
3. McArdle, W.D., Katch, F.I. & Katch, V.L. (2001). Exercise Physiology: Energy, Nutrition and Human Performance (5th ed.) (pp. 308-312, 347-355). Baltimore: Williams & Wilkins.

Maximal Oxygen Consumption

VO_2 max Criterion Test

Student Learning Objectives

After completing this lab, you should be able to:

1. Define, explain and correctly use key terms.
2. Explain how to administer an incremental exercise test to maximum.
3. Describe the heart rate, blood pressure and rate pressure product response to incremental aerobic exercise.
4. Explain why heart rate and rate of perceived exertion (RPE) can be used to determine exercise intensity.
5. List typical oxygen consumption values for rest, submaximal exercise and maximal exercise.

Equipment

- Heart Rate Watch/Transmitter Strap
- Lactate Analyzer and Accessories
- Motordriven Treadmill
- O_2 and CO_2 Analyzers
- Pneumoscan Flow Meter or Pneumotach
- RPE Scale
- Sphygmomanometer/Cuff/Stethoscope

Procedure

An incremental aerobic exercise test to maximum will be performed. One student volunteers or is selected. Either Protocol A or B may be utilized.

Protocols

Stand quietly on the treadmill. When gas analysis data indicates relaxation and a true resting state, 3 minutes of resting data are obtained. Gas analysis is continuous from that point.

A. Delta Efficiency and VO_2 max Protocol

Note to Instructor: Steps 1, 2 and 3 in Protocol A are included to allow calculation of delta efficiency for the Caloric Cost and Efficiency lab. These steps may be omitted if desired, except that Step 1 should be shortened to 1 minute, and the transition to 10% grade be made minute by minute with a 2% increase at the end of the first minute.

1. Walk at 3.5 $mi \cdot hr^{-1}$ at 0% grade for 5 minutes.
2. Sit and rest for 5 minutes.
3. Walk at 3.5 $mi \cdot hr^{-1}$ at 10% grade for 5 minutes.
4. Continue to maximal exertion:
   - Treadmill grade is elevated 1% each minute until 22% grade.
   - Treadmill speed remains constant at 3.5 $mi \cdot hr^{-1}$ until 22% grade when the speed is increased 0.5 $mi \cdot hr^{-1}$ every minute.
5. Oxygen consumption (VO_2), carbon dioxide production (VCO_2), respiratory exchange ratio (RER), heart rate (HR), blood pressure (BP), RPE and lactate ($[La^-]$) (optional) are measured and recorded as indicated in Data Table 1.0.

B. Alternate VO_2 max Protocol

1. Warm up with a 3 minute brisk walk (self-selected) at 5% grade followed by 3 minutes at the same load (or self-selected jogging pace) at 0% grade.
2. Speed remains constant, but grade is increased 1.5% each minute until volitional fatigue.[1]

Data Table 1.0: Incremental Exercise to Determine Maximal Oxygen Consumption

Name: ______________________ Age (yr): __________ Temp (°C): __________

Training Status: ______________________ Ht (cm): __________ P_B (mmHg): __________

Sex: ______________________ Wt (kg): __________ RH (%): __________

Speed ($mi \cdot hr^{-1}$) Grade (%)	Exercise Time (minutes)	VO_2* ($L \cdot min^{-1}$)	VCO_2 ($L \cdot min^{-1}$)	RER	HR ($b \cdot min^{-1}$)	BP (mmHg)	RPE	VO_2* ($mL \cdot kg^{-1} \cdot min^{-1}$)	[La^-] ($mmol \cdot L^{-1}$)
	Rest								
	Recovery								
	2								
	3								
	4								
	5								
	6								
	7								
	8								
	9								
	10								

* <u>*Note to Student*</u>*: Highlight or circle the subject's VO_2 max values in $L \cdot min^{-1}$ and $ml \cdot kg \cdot min^{-1}$.*

Student Activities

A. Definitions.

Define the following key terms. For those terms which are measurable variables, describe in your own words what they mean (not how they are obtained or calculated). Indicate the unit(s) of measurement.

1. Cardiac Output:

2. Fick Equation:

3. Incremental Aerobic Exercise to Maximum:

4. Maximal Heart Rate (HR max):

5. Maximal Oxygen Consumption (VO_2 max):

6. Minute Ventilation (V_E):

7. Oxygen Consumption (VO_2):

8. Rating of Perceived Exertion (RPE):

9. Stroke Volume (SV):

B. Analysis.

1. Graph the VO_2 response to the incremental portion of the treadmill test. Put VO_2 ($mL \cdot kg^{-1} \cdot min^{-1}$) on the Y-axis, and time and workrate (speed and grade) on the X-axis (see page 12 for an example of multiple units on an axis). Circle the value which you have identified as the subject's maximal VO_2.

2. Graph the HR response to the incremental portion of the treadmill test. Put HR on the Y-axis, and time and workrate (speed and grade) on the X-axis. Circle the value which you have identified as the subject's maximal HR.

3. Graph the blood pressure response to the incremental portion of the treadmill test. Put SBP and DBP on the Y-axis, and time and workrate (speed and grade) on the X-axis. Circle the value which you have identified as the subject's maximal SBP.

4. Graph HR and RPE versus VO_2 for the incremental portion of the treadmill test. Put HR on one Y-axis, RPE on a second Y-axis and VO_2 on the X-axis.

5. If not completed as part of the *Heart Rate and Blood Pressure* lab, calculate RPP for the incremental portion of the treadmill test.

C. Interpretation and Discussion.

1. State the theoretical criteria for determining whether or not a maximal VO_2 value has been obtained. Does this test meet these criteria? Support your answer.

2. What are the major cardiovascular determinants of VO_2 max? Find average values for these variables for the sex and appropriate age of the VO_2 max subject, calculate VO_2 max from them and compare them with the subject's VO_2 max results.

3. Explain why HR and RPE can be used to determine exercise intensity.

4. Using your graphs, explain why percent heart rate reserve (% HRR) equals percent oxygen consumption reserve (% VO_2 R) for many exercise modalities.

5. Using data from your *Heart Rate and Blood Pressure* lab (or theoretically, if these data are not available), compare and contrast the patterns of cardiovascular responses between aerobic and incremental resistance exercise.

D. Application.

1. Select one of the following age groups: a) 6-12 yr, b) 13-18 yr, c) 40-50 yr, or d) 60-70 yr. Using the actual VO_2 max achieved by the subject for an individual of the same sex, but in the age range you selected, explain how fit that fictional individual is.

2. Calculate the HR range that would provide the VO_2 max subject with a moderate workout. What would the oxygen consumption and treadmill setting be?

3. Why is a high VO_2 max good and/or important?

Reference

1. George, J.D., Stone, W.J., &Burkett, L.N. (1997). Non-exercise VO2 max estimation for physically active college students. Medicine and Science in Sport and Exercise, 29, 415-423.

Related Readings

1. Plowman, S.A. & Smith, D.L. (2003). Exercise Physiology for Health, Fitness and Performance (2nd ed.). San Francisco: Benjamin Cummings.
2. Powers, S.K. & Howley, E.T. (2001). Exercise Physiology: Theory and Application to Fitness and Performance (4th ed.) (pp. 279-285). Boston: McGraw-Hill.
3. McArdle, W.D., Katch, F.I. & Katch, V.L. (2001). Exercise Physiology: Energy, Nutrition and Human Performance (5th ed.) (pp. 160-163, 1119-1120). Baltimore: Williams & Wilkins.

Maximal Oxygen Consumption Field Test—PACER

Are the Estimated VO_2 max Results Affected by Agility?

Student Learning Objectives

After completing this lab, you should be able to:

1. Define, explain and correctly use key terms.
2. Describe the Progressive Aerobic Cardiovascular Endurance Run (PACER) test and explain why it can be used to predict maximal oxygen consumption (VO_2 max).
3. Describe a field test for assessing agility.
4. Explain the results of a correlation between agility and the PACER.

Equipment

- Cones/Tape Measure
- Heart Rate Watches/Transmitter Straps
- PACER Audio Tape or CD /Tape or CD Player
- Stopwatches

Procedure

A field test for agility and an endurance run to predict oxygen uptake will be performed. All students will be subjects.

> *Note to Student: Before coming to lab, complete the non-exercise prediction of VO_2 max questionnaire in Box 2.0.*

Protocols

A. Illinois Agility Run (IAR)[2]

Set-up: Mark two lines 30 feet apart with 4 cones equally spaced down the middle (Figure 1.0).

1. Warm up before the test, and practice the IAR course twice, once slowly and once fast.
2. Start from a prone position, hands at the side on the floor with palms up, just to the left of the first cone.
3. When instructed to "go," get up as fast as you can and sprint 30 feet.
4. Reverse at the 30 foot line drawn on the floor (at least one foot must touch or cross the line) and sprint back 30 feet to the start.
5. Turn left at top speed around cones.
6. Zig-zag left then right around the 4 cones making a right loop at top speed around the fourth cone.
7. Zig-zag right, left, right back around the 4 cones making a left turn at top speed around the last cone and sprint to the 30 foot line.
8. Perform the IAR twice, taking at least 2 minutes rest between trials. A partner times each run.
9. Record your best time in Data Table 1.0

B. Progressive Aerobic Cardiovascular Endurance Run (PACER)[1]

> *Note to Instructor: Information for obtaining the PACER CD is provided in Appendix B, or you can make your own tape.*

The PACER was developed as the 20 Meter Shuttle Test[3] to provide a means to test a large number of individuals to assess cardiorespiratory fitness and estimate oxygen uptake without needing a lot of space.

Figure 1.0
Illinois Agility Run (IAR) Course Diagram

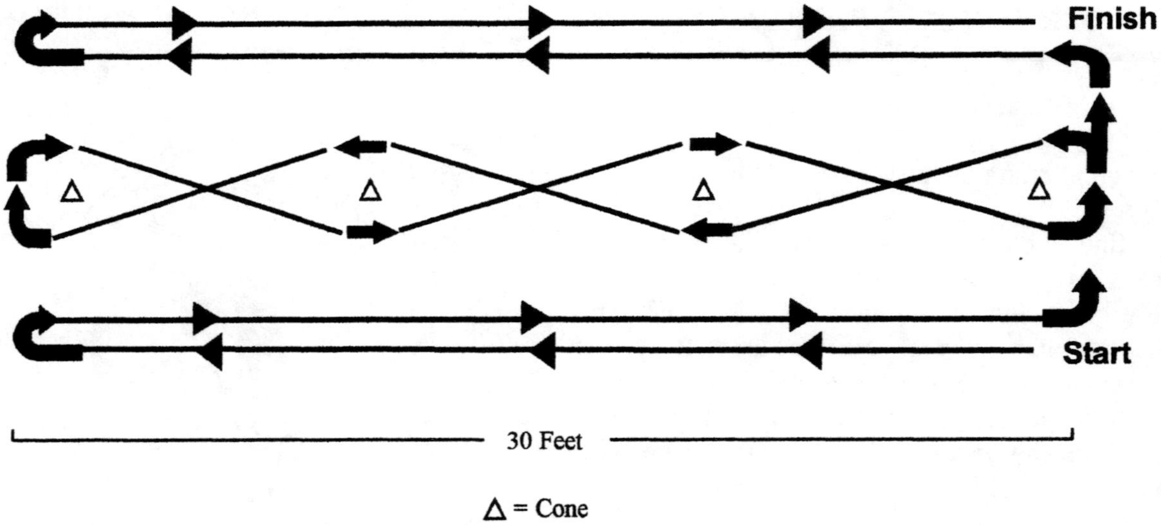

Set-up: Mark off a 20 meter long course as wide as needed or available.

1. Put on heart rate monitor, if available, and stand behind the line at one end of the 20 meter course.
2. When the PACER audio starts, activate the heart rate monitor, if available, and run 20 meters to the other line, timing the run to arrive when the next beep sounds (9 s).
3. Continue running at this speed (8.5 $km \cdot hr^{-1}$) to arrive at one line or the other each time there is a beep.
4. After each minute, the time interval between beeps will decrease so running speed needs to increase (0.5 $km \cdot hr^{-1}$ per stage). If the FITNESSGRAM® pre-recorded audio is being used, at the end of each shuttle there is a single beep, and at the end of each level (minute) there is a triple beep and a commentator identifies the level.
5. Always place one foot either on or behind the 20 meter mark at the end of each shuttle.

> *Note: If you arrive at the end of a shuttle before the beep sounds, turn around, wait for the beep and then resume running and adjust your speed.*

> *If you fail to reach the end of a shuttle before the beep sounds, you are allowed two or three further shuttles to attempt to regain the required pace before stopping.*

6. Run until you can no longer keep up with the speed set by the tape. At that point, read your heart rate (if no monitor is being worn, take an immediate post-exercise 6 second heart rate) and record in Data Table 1.0.
7. Record your PACER level and number of laps in in Box 1.0 and Data Table 1.0.

Data Table 1.0		
Height	_______ cm	_______ m
Weight	_______ kg	
BMI	_______	
Non-Exercise Prediction of VO_2 max	_______ $mL{\cdot}kg^{-1}{\cdot}min^{-1}$	
Illinois Agility Run (IAR) Time	_______ s	_______ classification
PACER Heart Rate	_______ $b{\cdot}min^{-1}$	
PACER	_______ level	_______ laps
PACER Predicted VO_2 max	_______ $mL{\cdot}kg^{-1}{\cdot}min^{-1}$	_______ classification

Box 1.0
PACER Data Sheet[1]

Level	Laps (Shuttles)*												*Speed ($km{\cdot}hr^{-1}$)*
1	1	2	3	4	5	6	7						*8.5*
2	8	9	10	11	12	13	14	15					*9.0*
3	16	17	18	19	20	21	22	23					*9.5*
4	24	25	26	27	28	29	30	31	32				*10.0*
5	33	34	35	36	37	38	39	40	41				*10.5*
6	42	43	44	45	46	47	48	49	50	51			*11.0*
7	52	53	54	55	56	57	58	59	60	61			*11.5*
8	62	63	64	65	66	67	68	69	70	71	72		*12.0*
9	73	74	75	76	77	78	79	80	81	82	83		*12.5*
10	84	85	86	87	88	89	90	91	92	93	94		*13.0*
11	95	96	97	98	99	100	101	102	103	104	105	106		*13.5*
12	107	108	109	110	111	112	113	114	115	116	117	118		*14.0*
13	119	120	121	122	123	124	124	126	127	128	129	130	131	*14.5*
14	132	133	134	135	136	137	138	139	140	141	142	143	144	*15.0*
15	145	146	147	148	149	150	151	152	153	154	155	156	157	*15.5*

* *Note to Student: Circle the number of shuttles completed.*

Reprinted with permission from the Cooper Institute for Aerobics Research, Dallas, TX. (Modified)

Box 2.0
Non-Exercise Prediction of VO_2 max Questionnaire

1. Determine your physical activity level using the **Code for Physical Activity**[3,5] below (0-7). Choose a number that best describes your physical activity for the previous month.

DID NOT PARTICIPATE REGULARLY IN PROGRAMMED RECREATION, SPORT OR HEAVY PHYSICAL ACTIVITY.
0—Avoided walking or exertion (e.g., always used elevator, drove whenever possible instead of walking).
1—Walked for pleasure, routinely used stairs, occasionally exercised sufficiently to cause heavy breathing or perspiration.

PARTICIPATED REGULARLY IN RECREATION OR WORK REQUIRING MODEST PHYSICAL ACTIVITY, SUCH AS GOLF, HORSEBACK RIDING, CALISTHENICS, GYMNASTICS, TABLE TENNIS, BOWLING, WEIGHTLIFTING OR YARD WORK.
2—10 to 60 minutes per week.
3—Over one hour per week.

PARTICIPATED REGULARLY IN HEAVY EXERCISE SUCH AS RUNNING OR JOGGING, SWIMMING, CYCLING, ROWING, SKIPPING ROPE, RUNNING IN PLACE OR ENGAGING IN VIGOROUS AEROBIC ACTIVITY TYPE EXERCISE SUCH AS TENNIS, BASKETBALL OR HANDBALL.
4—Ran less than one mile per week or spent less than 30 minutes per week in comparable physical activity.
5—Ran one to 5 miles per week or spent 30 to 60 minutes per week in comparable physical activity.
6—Ran 5 to 10 miles per week or spent 1 to 3 hours per week in comparable physical activity.
7—Ran over 10 miles per week or spent over 3 hours per week in comparable physical activity.

2. Calculate your BMI using the following equation: $\dfrac{\text{Weight (kg)}}{\text{Height (m}^2\text{)}}$

3. Using your activity code and BMI, calculate VO_2 max using equation A if you are **male** and equation B if you are **female**.
   A. VO_2 max ($mL \cdot kg^{-1} \cdot min^{-1}$) = 1.921(activity code) - .381(age in years) - .754(BMI) + 67.350
   B. VO_2 max ($mL \cdot kg^{-1} \cdot min^{-1}$) = 1.921(activity code) - .381(age in years) - .754(BMI) + 56.363

For Example:

- David claims his physical activity code is 3. He is 29 years old and his BMI is 24.
  VO_2 max ($mL \cdot kg^{-1} \cdot min^{-1}$) = 1.921(activity code) - .381(age in years) - .754(BMI) + 67.350
  = 1.921(3) - .381(29) - .754(24) + 67.350
  = 43.97
- Lisa claims her activity code is 5. She is 25 years old and her BMI is 20.
  VO_2 max ($mL \cdot kg^{-1} \cdot min^{-1}$) = 1.921(activity code) - .381(age in years) - .754(BMI) + 56.363
  = 1.921(5) - .381(25) - .754(20) + 56.363
  = 41.36

Box 3.0
Prediction of VO_2 max from the PACER

1. Estimate your maximum oxygen consumption (VO_2 max) from the PACER test using the following equation:[4]

Estimated VO_2 max ($mL \cdot kg^{-1} \cdot min^{-1}$) = -23.4 + 5.8 (x)

Where x is the maximal speed in $km \cdot hr^{-1}$ based on the level achieved during the PACER (Box 1.0)

For example:

- David stopped the PACER at level 13 (which corresponds to a speed of 14.5 $km \cdot hr^{-1}$)

  VO_2 ($mL \cdot kg^{-1} \cdot min^{-1}$) = -23.4 + 5.8 (14.5)

  = -23.4 + 84.1

  = 60.7

Data Table 2.0

Subject	Sex	Activity Level (Box 2.0)	Illinois Agility Run (s)	Measured VO_2 max Treadmill Test ($mL \cdot kg^{-1} \cdot min^{-1}$)*	Estimated VO_2 max ($mL \cdot kg^{-1} \cdot min^{-1}$)	
					PACER	Non-Exercise Questionnaire
1						
2						
3						
4.						
5						
6						
7						
8						
9						
10						
11						
12						
13						
14						
15						
16						
17						
18						
19						
20						
Mean						
SD						

* *Note to Instructor: Only those students who were also subjects for the Maximal Oxygen Consumption lab will have data for this column*

Student Activities

A. Definitions.

Define the following key terms. For those terms which are measurable variables, describe in your own words what they mean (not how they are obtained or calculated). Indicate the unit(s) of measurement.

1. Agility:

2. Criterion Test:

3. Field Test:

4. Maximal Oxygen Consumption (VO_2 max):

B. Analysis.

1. Complete the non-exercise prediction of VO_2 max questionnaire using Box 2.0 and record in Data Table 1.0.

2. Using the speed ($km \cdot hr^{-1}$) that corresponds to the level you achieved for the PACER, calculate your PACER predicted VO_2 max using Box 3.0 and record in Data Table 1.0.

3. Using Appendix A, find your classification for your IAR time, non-exercise predicted VO_2 max, and PACER predicted VO_2 max and record in Data Table 1.0.

Note to Instructor: For questions 4, 5, 6 and 7, students can individually compute or be given correlation coefficients for all data. Alternatively, students may be asked to construct scattergrams.

4. Using the class data in Data Table 2.0, compute a correlation coefficient between the IAR time and the PACER predicted VO_2 max.

5. Using the class data in Data Table 2.0, compute a correlation coefficient between the PACER predicted VO_2 max and the VO_2 max predicted from the non-exercise questionnaire.

6. Using class data in Data Table 2.0, compute a correlation coefficient between activity level and the PACER predicted VO_2 max.

7. If a sufficient number of students have a VO_2 max that was directly measured in the *Maximal Oxygen Consumption* lab, compute a correlation between the measured VO_2 max and each of the predicted VO_2 max values recorded in Data Table 2.0.

C. Interpretation and Discussion.

1. State how you would expect agility to be related to performance on the PACER. Provide your reasoning. Did the results of this lab support your expectations? Explain.

2. Discuss the results of the scattergrams and/or correlational analyses (Section B, 4, 5, 6 and 7).

3. Discuss the relationship between physical activity and aerobic fitness a) theoretically and b) using the results of the correlational analysis between the activity level score and the PACER predicted VO_2 max.

4. Contrast and discuss the relationship between endurance performance (such as the PACER) and VO_2 max between children/adolescents and adults.

5. The following variables are the major determinants of VO_2 max:
   - Cardiac Output (Q) (heart rate x stroke volume)
   - Arterio-Venous Oxygen Difference (a-vO_2 diff)
   - Heart Size and Volume
   - Hemoglobin (Hb) Level
   - Mitochondrial Density

   a. Define each variable and indicate what differences, if any, exist between one of the following pair of populations:

      - males and females
      - children/adolescents and middle-aged adults of one sex
      - middle-aged adults and elderly of one sex

   b. Give representative values for each of the variables at rest and at maximal exercise. Theoretically, how should these differences influence VO_2 max?

   c. Two of the variables are related mathmatically by the Fick Equation. Find this equation and, using the representative values you have presented for maximal exercise, show mathmatically the difference in VO_2 max for the population pair you selected.

D. Application.

1. Would improving your agility have an effect on your PACER score? Defend your answer.

2. Would increasing your activity level have an effect on your PACER score? Defend your answer.

References

1. Cooper Institute for Aerobic Research (1999). FITNESSGRAM Test Administration Manual (2nd ed.). Champaign, IL: Human Kinetics.
2. Cureton, T.K., Jr. (1970). Physical Fitness Workbook for Adults (p. 120). Champaign, IL: Stipes Publishing Co.
3. Jackson, A.S., Blair, S.N., Mahar, M.T., Wier, L.T., Ross, R.M. & Stutesville, J.E. (1990). Prediction of functional aerobic capacity without exercise testing. Medicine and Science in Sport and Exercise, 22, 863-870.
4. Lèger, L.A., Mercier, D., Gadoury, C., & Lambert, J. (1988). The multistage 20 metre shuttle run test for aerobic fitness. Journal of Sport Science, 6, 93-101.
5. Ross, R.M. & Jackson, A.S. (1990). Exercise Concepts, Calculations and Computer Applications (pp. 95-103, 109). Carmel, IN: Benchmark Press.

Related Readings

1. Plowman, S.A. & Smith, D.L. (2003). Exercise Physiology for Health, Fitness and Performance (2nd ed.). San Francisco: Benjamin Cummings.
2. Powers, S.K. & Howley, E.T. (2001). Exercise Physiology: Theory and Application to Fitness and Performance (4th ed.) (pp. 276-279). Boston: McGraw-Hill.
3. McArdle, W.D., Katch, F.I. & Katch, V.L. (2001). Exercise Physiology: Energy, Nutrition and Human Performance (5th ed.) (pp. 240-246). Baltimore: Williams & Wilkins.

The Influence of Fluid Replacement During Long-Term Exercise

Does it Impact Cardiovascular Response?

Student Learning Objectives

After completing this lab, you should be able to:

1. Define, explain and correctly use key terms.
2. Compare and contrast the cardiovascular exercise response to long-term submaximal aerobic exercise with and without fluid replacement.

Equipment

- Cycle Ergometer, Stair Stepper Treadmill (or other aerobic equipment)
- Heart Rate Watches/Transmitter Straps
- Spygmomanometer/Cuff/Stethoscope
- Tympanic or Rectal Temperature Probe or Thermistors (optional)
- Water/Water Bottle

Procedure

The cardiovascular response to long-term aerobic exercise with and without fluid replacement will be examined. Determine which students will be subjects. Suggestions:

- The same student or all students perform both protocols, in which case at least 24 hours should separate exercise days.
- Two different students of equal training status each perform one of the protocols.
- The instructor divides the class into two groups: non-fluid replacement and fluid replacement. In this case, the order of the trials, fluid/no fluid, should be randomized. Group data would be compared in the analysis section.
- Pairs of students (as subject and experimenter) could use different exercise equipment simultaneously.

If students are completing both protocols, at least 24 hours should separate test days, and care should be taken to administer the exercise tests under similar conditions (i.e., same or similar clothing, time of day, etc.). Use the 24 hour inventory in *Appendix C* to check this. If students do both tests, randomize the order.

Protocols

Note to Instructor: The measurement of body temperature is optional. If gas analysis is included for the non-fluid replacement trial, it can be used as Protocol B in the Responses to Different Categories of Exercise lab.

Select and prepare exercise equipment.

A. Non-Fluid Replacement

1. Select a workrate that will elicit a heart rate of 135-140 b·min^{-1} within the first 5 minutes of exercise, or utilize the same workrate from the fluid replacement trial.
2. Record workrate in Data Table 1.0.
3. Sustain this workrate for 50 to 120 minutes without drinking fluids.
4. Heart rate (HR), blood pressure (BP), rating of perceived exertion (RPE) and, if available, body temperature are measured and recorded as

indicated in Data Table 1.0.

B. Fluid Replacement

1. Select a workrate that will elicit a heart rate of 135-140 b·min^{-1} within the first 5 minutes of exercise, or utilize the same workrate from the non-fluid replacement trial.
2. Record workrate in Data Table 2.0.
3. Sustain workrate for 50 to 120 minutes, drinking 200-400 ml of water every 15 minutes.
4. HR, BP, RPE and, if available, body temperature are measured and recorded as indicated in Data Table 2.0.

Data Table 1.0: Non-Fluid Replacement

Name: ______________________ Age (yr): __________ Temp (°C): __________

Training Status: ______________________ Ht (cm): __________ P_B (mmHg): __________

Sex: ______________________ Wt (kg): __________ RH (%): __________

Workrate: ______________________ (@ 135-140 b·min^{-1}) Circle: T_1 T_2

Time (minutes)	HR (b·min^{-1})	BP (mmHg)	RPE	Body Temperature (°C) (optional)
Rest				
5				
10				
15				
20				
25				
30				
35				
40				
45				
50				
55				
60				
65				
70				
75				
80				
85				
90				
95				
100				
105				
110				
115				
120				

Data Table 2.0: Fluid Replacement

Name:	______________	Age (yr):	______	Temp (°C):	______
Training Status:	______________	Ht (cm):	______	P_B (mmHg):	______
Sex:	______________	Wt (kg):	______	RH (%):	______
Workrate:	______________	(@ 135-140 b·min^{-1})		Circle:	T_1 T_2

Time (minutes)	HR (b·min^{-1})	BP (mmHg)	RPE	Body Temperature (°C) (optional)
Rest				
5				
10				
15				
20				
25				
30				
35				
40				
45				
50				
55				
60				
65				
70				
75				
80				
85				
90				
95				
100				
105				
110				
115				
120				

Student Activities

A. Definitions.

Define the following key terms. For those terms which are measurable variables, describe in your own words what they mean (not how they are obtained or calculated). Indicate the unit(s) of measurement.

1. Cardiovascular Drift:

2. Dehydration:

3. Thermal Regulation:

B. Analysis.

1. Graph the HR response to exercise with and without fluid replacement. Place heart rate on the Y-axis and time on the X-axis.

2. Graph the SBP and DBP response to exercise with and without fluid replacement. Place blood pressure on the Y-axis and time on the X-axis.

3. Graph the RPE response to exercise with and without fluid replacement. Place RPE on the Y-axis and time on the X-axis.

4. If available, graph the body temperature response to exercise with and without fluid replacement. Place body temperature on the Y-axis and time on the X-axis.

C. Interpretation and Discussion.

1. On the basis of your data, what is the impact of fluid replacement on the cardiovascular response to moderate, long-term submaximal aerobic exercise?

2. What are the physiological explanations which account for the differences observed during exercise with and without fluid replacement?

D. Application.

1. How do exercise intensity and duration affect the need for replacing fluid lost during exercise?

2. Discuss the merits of fluid replacement using water versus "sports drinks" at varying intensities and durations of exercise.

Related Readings

1. Plowman, S.A. & Smith, D.L. (2003). Exercise Physiology for Health, Fitness and Performance (2nd ed.). San Francisco: Benjamin Cummings.
2. Powers, S.K. & Howley, E.T. (2001). Exercise Physiology: Theory and Application to Fitness and Performance (4th ed.) (pp. 445-448). Boston: McGraw-Hill.
3. McArdle, W.D., Katch, F.I. & Katch, V.L. (2001). Exercise Physiology: Energy, Nutrition and Human Performance (5th ed.) (pp. 75-77, 97-102). Baltimore: Williams & Wilkins.

Cardiovascular Exercise Responses to Varying Temperature and Humidity

Hot (Wet and/or Dry), Cold and Thermoneutral

Student Learning Objectives

After completing this lab, you should be able to:

1. Define, explain and correctly use key terms.
2. Compare and contrast the effects of different thermal environments on the cardiovascular response to submaximal aerobic exercise.

Equipment

- Cycle Ergometer, Stair Stepper, Rowing Machine (or other portable exercise equipment)
- Environmental Chamber (optional)
- Heart Rate Watches/Transmitter Straps
- Scale
- Sphygmomanometer/Cuff/Stethoscope
- Tympanic or Rectal Temperature Probe or Thermistors (optional)

Procedure

The cardiovascular response to short-term exercise in three different thermal environments will be examined: a thermoneutral environment, a hot environment and a cold environment. Determine which students will be subjects. Suggestions:

- The same student or all students perform all three protocols, in which case at least 24 hours should separate exercise days.
- Three different students of equal training status each perform one of the three protocols.
- One male and one female of equal training status perform all three protocols.
- Two or three students of the same sex but different training status (non-exerciser, aerobically trained, resistance trained) perform all three protocols.

If students are completing both protocols, at least 24 hours should separate test days, and care should be taken to administer the exercise tests under similar conditions (i.e, same or similar clothing, time of day, etc.). Use the 24 hour inventory to check this (*Appendix C*).

Protocol

Note to Instructor: Complete the exercise in the thermoneutral environment first. If students are doing both tests, randomize the order of the Hot and Cold Environment trials. The measurement of body temperature is optional.

Select and prepare exercise equipment.

A. Thermoneutral Environment

Suggested Location: Laboratory or other thermoneutral environment.

1. Record environmental conditions of the testing area in Data Table 1.0.
2. Select a workrate that will elicit a heart rate of 150-160 b·min^{-1} within the first 5 minutes of exercise.
3. Record the workrate in Data Table 1.0.
4. Exercise for 30 minutes without fluid/fuel

replacement.

5. Heart rate (HR), blood Pressure (BP), rating of perceived exertion (RPE) and body temperature are measured and recorded as indicated in Data Table 1.0.

B. <u>Hot Environment</u>

Suggested Location: On deck beside a pool, in a furnace room or in an environmental chamber.

> <u>Note to Instructor</u>: *If you have an environmental chamber, another option would be to do **both** a hot-dry and a hot-humid condition.*

1. Record environmental conditions of the testing area in Data Table 2.0.
2. Exercise for 30 minutes without fluid/fuel replacement at the same workrate used in Protocol A.

> <u>Note</u>: *If different students are used for the different conditions, the same **relative** workrate should be used.*

3. HR, BP, RPE and body temperature are measured and recorded as indicated in Data Table 2.0.

C. <u>Cold Environment</u>

Suggested Location: Outside, depending on the season (weather permitting), or in extreme air conditioning.

1. Record environmental conditions of the testing area in Data Table 3.0.
2. Exercise for 30 minutes without fluid/fuel replacement at the same workrate used in Protocol A.

> <u>Note</u>: *If different students are used for the different conditions, the same **relative** workrate should be used.*

3. HR, BP, RPE and body temperature are measured and recorded as indicated in Data Table 3.0.

Data Table 1.0: Thermoneutral Environment

Name: ______________________ Age (yr): __________ Temp (°C): __________

Training Status: ______________________ Ht (cm): __________ P_B (mmHg): __________

Sex: ______________________ Wt (kg): __________ RH (%): __________

Workrate at HR of 150-160 b·min^{-1}: ______________________

Time (minutes)	HR (b·min^{-1})	BP (mmHg)	RPE	Body Temperature (°C) (optional)
0				
1				
2				
3				
4				
5				
6				
7				
8				
9				
10				
11				
12				
13				
14				
15				
16				
17				
18				
19				
20				
21				
22				
23				
24				
25				
26				
27				
28				
29				
30				

Data Table 2.0: Hot Environment

Name: ______________ Age (yr): ________ Temp (°C): ________

Training Status: ______________ Ht (cm): ________ P_B (mmHg): ________

Sex: ______________ Wt (kg): ________ RH (%): ________

Thermoneutral Workrate: ______________ Circle: wet dry

Time (minutes)	HR ($b \cdot min^{-1}$)	BP (mmHg)	RPE	Body Temperature (°C) (optional)
0				
1				
2				
3				
4				
5				
6				
7				
8				
9				
10				
11				
12				
13				
14				
15				
16				
17				
18				
19				
20				
21				
22				
23				
24				
25				
26				
27				
28				
29				
30				

Data Table 3.0: Cold Environment

Name: ____________________ Age (yr): __________ Temp (°C): __________

Training Status: ____________________ Ht (cm): __________ P_B (mmHg): __________

Sex: ____________________ Wt (kg): __________ RH (%): __________

Thermoneutral Workrate: ______________________________

Time (minutes)	HR (b·min^{-1})	BP (mmHg)	RPE	Body Temperature (°C) (optional)
0				
1				
2				
3				
4				
5				
6				
7				
8				
9				
10				
11				
12				
13				
14				
15				
16				
17				
18				
19				
20				
21				
22				
23				
24				
25				
26				
27				
28				
29				
30				

Student Activities

A. Definitions.

Define the following key terms. For those terms which are measurable variables, describe in your own words what they mean (not how they are obtained or calculated). Indicate the unit(s) of measurment.

1. Acclimatization:

2. Heat Stress Index:

3. Hyperthermia:

4. Hypothermia:

5. Sweat Rate:

6. Thermoneutral:

B. Analysis.

1. Graph the HR response to the exercise performed in different thermal environments. Place HR on the Y-axis and time on the X-axis.

2. Graph the blood pressure response to the exercise performed in different thermal environments. Place SBP and DBP on the Y-axis and time on the X-axis.

3. Graph the RPE response to the exercise performed in different thermal environments. Place RPE on the Y-axis and time on the X-axis.

4. Graph the relationship between HR and RPE to the exercise performed in different thermal environments. Place RPE on the Y-axis and HR on the X-axis.

5. If available, graph the body temperature response to the exercise performed in different thermal environments. Place body temperature on the Y-axis and time on the X-axis

C. Interpretation and Discussion.

1. Discuss the different responses observed during the same exercise in different thermal environments. Do your results support what is generally known about exercise under different environmental conditions? Before writing the discussion, state whether your test was done in hot-humid or hot-dry conditions.

2. What are the physiological mechanisms which account for the differences observed during exercise in different thermal environments?

3. How is the HR-RPE relationship affected by different thermal environments?

D. Application.

1. On the basis of this laboratory, what advice would you give an endurance athlete from Green Bay, WI who will be training in the heat and humidity of Florida while on vacation there in July?

Related Readings

1. Plowman, S.A. & Smith, D.L. (2003). Exercise Physiology for Health, Fitness and Performance (2nd ed.). San Francisco: Benjamin Cummings.
2. Powers, S.K. & Howley, E.T. (2001). Exercise Physiology: Theory and Application to Fitness and Performance (4th ed.) (pp. 229-233). Boston: McGraw-Hill.
3. McArdle, W.D., Katch, F.I. & Katch, V.L. (2001). Exercise Physiology: Energy, Nutrition and Human Performance (5th ed.) (pp. 633-638, 647-650). Baltimore: Williams & Wilkins.

Muscular Fiber Typing

The Relationship Between Fiber Type, VO_2 max and Fatigue

Student Learning Objectives

After completing this lab, you should be able to:

1. Define, explain and correctly use key terms.
2. Explain how the proportion of fast and slow twitch muscle fibers of the quadriceps is related to muscle force production, aerobic fitness and fatigue.
3. Describe a method of predicting proportion of fast twitch muscle fibers from an isokinetic fatigue test.
4. Relate the production of lactate to fiber type.

Equipment

- Isokinetic Dynamometer
- Lactate Analyzer and Acessories

Procedure

The proportion of fast twitch and slow twitch muscle fibers will be predicted from an isokinetic fatigue test. All students will be subjects; students should work with a partner and test each other.

Protocol

Note to Instructor: The measurement of blood lactate concentrations in this lab is optional.

1. Obtain a pre-exercise lactate measurement and record in Data Table 1.0.
2. Warm up by riding the cycle ergometer for 5 minutes (1 kp for females and 2 kp for males at 50-60 rev·min^{-1}) and statically stretch the hamstrings and quadriceps.
3. Follow the instructions for calibrating and performing a test for the isokinetic dynamometer you will be using.
4. Your partner should make sure you are properly positioned on the dynamometer. Typically, when testing leg extension and flexion, you should be seated with your back at an angle of 100°, and the dynamometer shaft should be lined up with the axis of rotation of your knee joint. If not, adjust either your position or the dynamometer.
5. Practice on the isokinetic dynamometer by doing 6-10 reciprocal contractions of the quadriceps at 120°·sec^{-1}, gradually increasing the intensity.
6. Rest for 1-2 minutes.
7. Perform 50 leg extensions as hard and as fast as possible. After each leg extension, flex the hamstrings just hard enough to return to the starting position in about 2 seconds. It is important that each contraction is maximal and that you do not attempt to pace yourself.
8. Record the peak torque for contractions 1, 2, 3, 48, 49 and 50 in Data Table 1.0.
9. Cool down by riding the cycle ergometer for 3 minutes.
10. Obtain a post-exercise lactate measurement and record in Data Table 1.0.

Data Table 1.0	
Pre-Exercise Lactate ($mmol \cdot L^{-1}$)	
Contractions	Peak Torque
1	
2	
3	
Mean	
Contractions	Peak Torque
48	
49	
50	
Mean	
Post-Exercise Lactate ($mmol \cdot L^{-1}$)	

Data Table 2.0

Subject	PT[1]	FPT[2]	BW[3]	PT/BW[4]	% FT	% ST	VO_2 max[5]	FI[6]	$[La^-]$[7]
1									
2									
3									
4									
5									
6									
7									
8									
9									
10									
11									
12									
13									
14									
15									
Mean									
SD									

[1]Initial Peak torque: Average of contractions 1, 2 and 3. [2]Final Peak Torque: Average of contractions 48, 49 and 50. [3]Body weight in kilograms. [4]Peak torque divided by body weight in kilograms. [5]VO_2 max estimated from the PACER lab. [6]Fatigue index from the *Lactate Responses* lab. [7]Post-exercise - pre-exercise.

Student Activities

A. Definitions.

Define the following key terms. For those terms which are measurable variables, describe in your own words what they mean (not how they are obtained or calculated). Indicate the unit(s) of measurement.

1. Fast Glycolytic (FG):

2. Fast Oxidative Glycolytic (FOG):

3. Slow Oxidative (SO):

4. Type I:

5. Type IIA:

6. Type IIB:

B. Analysis.

1. Estimate the fiber type distribution for each person in your lab section using the following equations and record in Data Table 2.0.

   Fast Twitch Fiber (%) = 0.9 (x) + 5.2[1]

   Where:
   x = [(initial peak torque - final peak torque) ÷ initial peak torque] x 100
   initial peak torque = the mean of contractions 1, 2 and 3
   final peak torque = the mean of contractions 48, 49 and 50.

   Slow Twitch Fiber % = 100% - Fast Twitch Fiber %

2. Using the class data in Data Table 2.0, create a scattergram showing the relationship between peak torque (PT) and relative proportion of fast twitch fibers (% FT).

3. Using class data in Data Table 2.0, create a scattergram showing the relationship between peak torque/ body weight (PT/BW) and proportion of fast twitch fibers (% FT).

4. Using class data in Data Table 2.0, create a scattergram illustrating the relationship between proportion of fast twitch fibers (% FT) and lactate concentration ($[La^-]$).

5. Using the VO_2 max data from the PACER lab, create a scattergram illustrating the relationship between estimated VO_2 max and proportion of slow twitch muscle fibers (% ST).

6. Using the fatigue index data from the *Lactate Responses* lab 30 second Wingate Anaerobic Test, create a scattergram illustrating the relationship between proportion of slow twitch muscle fibers (% ST) and the fatigue index (FI)

C. Interpretation and Discussion.

1. Based on each of your scattergrams, what conclusions can you draw regarding the relationships illustrated? Does the literature support your conclusions? If not, what are some reasons that might explain the discrepancy?

D. Application.

1. Using the values 20% FT, 40% FT, 60% FT and 80% FT, select sports or events in which individuals with each fiber type composition would be genetically predisposed to succeed.

Reference

1. Thortenson, A.T. & Karlsson, J. (1976). Fatiguability and Fibre Composition of Human Skeletal Muscle. Acta Physiologica Scandinavica, 98, 318-322.

Related Readings

1. Plowman, S.A. & Smith, D.L. (2003). Exercise Physiology for Health, Fitness and Performance (2nd ed.). San Francisco: Benjamin Cummings.
2. Powers, S.K. & Howley, E.T. (2001). Exercise Physiology: Theory and Application to Fitness and Performance (4th ed.) (pp. 139-142). Boston: McGraw-Hill.
3. McArdle, W.D., Katch, F.I. & Katch, V.L. (2001). Exercise Physiology: Energy, Nutrition and Human Performance (5th ed.) (pp. 374-380). Baltimore: Williams & Wilkins.

Muscle Physiology

Dynamic and Static Contractions

Student Learning Objectives

After completing this lab, you should be able to:

1. Describe, explain and correctly use key terms.
2. Describe how joint angle, muscle length and speed of limb movement affect the force output of a muscle.
3. Calculate the flexor/extensor torque ratio for a knee joint.

Equipment

- Equipment to Measure Leg Strength Statically (strain gauges, cable tensionmeter, other dynamometers).
- Isokinetic Dynamometer

Procedure

The effect of joint angle, muscle length and speed of limb movement on the force output of the quadriceps muscle will be examined. All students will be subjects; students should work with a partner and test each other. Half of the class should begin by performing static contractions, while the other half should start by doing dynamic contractions.

Protocols

Warm up by riding the cycle ergometer for 5 minutes (1 kp for females and 2 kp for males) and stretching the hamstrings and quadriceps.

A. Dynamic Contractions

1. Follow the instructions for calibrating and performing a test for the isokinetic dynamometer you will be using.
2. A partner should check to make sure you are properly positioned on the dynamometer. Typically, when testing leg extension and flexion, you should be seated with your back at an angle of 100°, and the dynamometer shaft should be lined up with the axis of rotation of your knee joint. If not, adjust either your position or the dynamometer.
3. Warm up by doing 6-10 reciprocal contractions of the quadriceps at $120°\cdot sec^{-1}$, gradually increasing the intensity.
4. Perform 4 reciprocal contractions of the quadriceps and hamstrings as hard and fast as possible at $30°\cdot sec^{-1}$.
5. Record the peak torque from the 3 highest contractions for extension (Ext) and flexion (Flex) in Data Table 1.0A.
6. Repeat steps 4 and 5 at speeds of $120°\cdot sec^{-1}$, $210°\cdot sec^{-1}$ and $300°\cdot sec^{-1}$.
7. Following the strength tests, perform a fatigue test by doing as many contractions as possible in 60 seconds at a speed of $120°\cdot sec^{-1}$, contracting as hard and as fast as possible — no pacing.
8. Record initial and final torque of fatigue test in Data Table 1.0A.

B. Static Contractions

1. Follow the instructions for calibrating and performing a test for the equipment you are using to measure static strength.
2. A partner should secure a cable so that your

knee is fixed at an angle of ≈ 75° (inside angle between femur and tibia).

3. Warm up by doing 3 submaximal static contractions of the quadriceps, gradually increasing the intensity.
4. Contract the quadriceps maximally, attempting to extend the leg to 180°.
5. Rest for 1 minute and perform the trial again.
6. Record the peak force from the two separate contractions in Data Table 2.0A.
7. Repeat steps 4-6 at angles approximating 100°, 125°, 150° and 175°.

Note: The angles may be randomized.

8. Following the strength tests, perform a fatigue test by maximally contracting the quadriceps for 60 seconds at an knee angle of 100°.
9. Record intial and final forces of fatigue test in Data Table 2.0A.

Data Table 1.0A Dyanamic Contractions									
Subject:________________________					Unit of Measure:______________				
Velocity	Contraction #1		Contraction #2		Contraction #3		Average		Flex/Ext Ratio
	Ext	Flex	Ext	Flex	Ext	Flex	Ext	Flex	
$30^{o}\cdot s^{-1}$									
$120^{o}\cdot s^{-1}$									
$210^{o}\cdot s^{-1}$									
$300^{o}\cdot s^{-1}$									

Dynamic Contractions Fatigue Test		
	60 s Initial Torque Reading	60 s Final Torque Reading
$120^{o}\cdot s^{-1}$		

Data Table 1.0B Mean Extension Torque and Flexor/Extensor Ratio for Each Subject at Each Speed								
Subject	Peak Extension Torque				Flexor/Extensor Ratio			
	$30^{o}\cdot sec^{-1}$	$120^{o}\cdot sec^{-1}$	$210^{o}\cdot sec^{-1}$	$300^{o}\cdot sec^{-1}$	$30^{o}\cdot sec^{-1}$	$120^{o}\cdot sec^{-1}$	$210^{o}\cdot sec^{-1}$	$300^{o}\cdot sec^{-1}$
1								
2								
3								
4								
5								
6								
7								
8								
9								
10								
11								
12								
13								
14								
15								
16								
17								
18								
19								
20								
Mean								
SD								

Data Table 2.0A Static Contraction			
Subject:______________________			Unit of measure:______________
Angle	Contraction #1	Contraction #2	Average force

Static Contraction Fatigue Test		
Lever Arm Length: ______________		
Angle	60 s Initial Force Reading	60 s Final Force Reading

Data Table 2.0B Mean Force, 60 s Peak Force and 60 s Final Force for Each Subject at Each Angle							
Subject	Angle					Fatigue Test	
	75°	100°	125°	150°	175°	60 s Peak Force	60 s Final Force
1							
2							
3							
4							
5							
6							
7							
8							
9							
10							
11							
12							
13							
14							
15							
16							
17							
18							
19							
20							
Mean							
SD							

Student Activities

A. Definitions.

Define the following key terms. For those terms which are measurable variables, describe in your own words what they mean (not how they are obtained or calculated). Indicate the unit(s) of measurement.

1. Flexor-Extensor Torque Ratio:

2. Force-Velocity Relationship:

3. Isokinetic:

4. Length-Tension Relationship:

5. Static:

B. Analysis.

1. Using the data in Data Table 1.0A, calculate the flexor/extensor ratios by dividing the mean peak torque for flexion by the mean peak torque for extension for each velocity.

2. Using the class data from Data Table 1.0B, create a line graph with velocity on the X-axis and torque on the Y-axis and plot the mean extension torque values generated during the dynamic contractions for each velocity tested. In addition, select one individual, yourself if possible, and plot the same data on the same graph.

3. Using the class data from Data Table 1.0B, create a line graph with velocity on the X-axis and the flexor/extensor torque ratio on the Y-axis and plot the mean flexor/extensor ratios calculated for each velocity tested. In addition, select one individual, yourself if possible, and plot the same data on the same graph.

4. Using the class data from Data Table 2.0B, create a line graph with angle on the X-axis and force on the Y-axis and plot the mean force generated statically at each angle tested for the static contractions. In addition, select one individual, yourself if possible, and plot the same data on the same graph.

5. Select one subject, yourself if you did this test, and calculate the dynamic strength decrement index using the equation below. Use the initial and final extension torque values generated during the 60 second fatigue test (Data Table 1.0A).

$$\left[\frac{\text{highest dynamic force - lowest dynamic force}}{\text{highest dynamic force}}\right] \times 100 = \_\_\_\_\_\_ \%$$

6. Select one subject, yourself if you did this test, and calculate the static strength decrement index using the equation below. Use the initial and final extension forces generated during the 60 second fatigue test (Data Table 2.0A).

$$\left[\frac{\text{highest static force - lowest static force}}{\text{highest static force}}\right] \times 100 = \_\_\_\_\_\_ \%$$

7. Select one subject, yourself if you did the test, and calculate the difference in strength between the static and dynamic contractions using the equation below. For the static test, use the force generated at 100° and convert to Newton-meters (first convert kilograms to Newtons, then multiply by lever arm length in meters). For the dynamic force, use the average extension torque generated at $210°\cdot sec^{-1}$.

$$\left[\frac{\text{static peak force - dynamic peak force}}{\text{static peak force}}\right] \times 100 = \_\_\_\_\_\_ \%$$

C. Interpretation and Discussion.

1. Theoretically, how does the speed of limb movement affect peak torque generated? Describe how the lab data supports or refutes this basic relationship.

2. Theoretically, how does peak force generated change with a change in the length of the quadriceps? Describe how the lab data supports or refutes this basic relationship.

D. Application.

1. How can you apply the information in this lab?

Related Readings

1. Plowman, S.A. & Smith, D.L. (2003). Exercise Physiology for Health, Fitness and Performance (2nd ed.). San Francisco: Benjamin Cummings.
2. Powers, S.K. & Howley, E.T. (2001). Exercise Physiology: Theory and Application to Fitness and Performance (4th ed.) (pp. 399-402). Boston: McGraw-Hill.
3. McArdle, W.D., Katch, F.I. & Katch, V.L. (2001). Exercise Physiology: Energy, Nutrition and Human Performance (5th ed.) (pp. 519-524). Baltimore: Williams & Wilkins.

Relationship Between Muscular Strength and Muscular Endurance

Absolute and Relative Muscular Endurance

Student Learning Objectives

After completing this lab, you should be able to:

1. Define, explain and correctly use key terms.
2. Distinguish between absolute muscular endurance and relative muscular endurance.
3. Explain the theoretical relationship between muscular strength and relative muscular endurance and between muscular strength and absolute muscular endurance.

Equipment

- Bench Press Bench and Rack
- Hip Sled
- Lat-Pull Down Machine (preferably a plate-loaded machine)
- Olympic Barbell
- Other Equipment (for lifts chosen by the instructor)
- Weight Plates

Procedure

The relationship between strength and absolute muscular endurance and between strength and relative muscular endurance will be assessed using the following exercises: bench press, lat-pull down and leg press. All students will be subjects; students should work with a partner and test each other. While students do not need to have prior experience lifting, experience with the lifts used can improve accuracy of measurement and reduce the risk of developing delayed onset muscle soreness. It is recommended that students practice the lifts, including proper spotting techniques, for at least two weeks prior to completing this lab. See Box 1.0 for the procedures for performing the bench press, leg press and lat-pull down exercises.

Note to Instructor: This lab can be completed using the lifts described or any other lifts you which to substitute or include.

Protocols

A. Muscular Strength - 1 Repetition Maximum (1 RM) Assessment

1. Warm up with 6-10 repetitions using a moderate amount of weight (either ≈ 90% of the weight you normally work out with, or an estimated amount): Your partner spots the lift.
2. Increase the load by 5-90 pounds, depending on the exercise, and perform 2 repetitions: Your partner spots the lift.
3. Rest for 1-2 minutes
4. Increase the load by 5-90 pounds, depending on the exercise, and perform 1 repetition: Your partner spots the lift.
5. Rest for 1-2 minutes.
6. Repeat steps 4 and 5 until a weight is reached that cannot be lifted with good form. If you come close to lifting the weight, follow that set with either the same weight or a load slightly lighter.
7. Rotate stations and determine your 1 RM for all muscle groups being investigated.
8. Record 1 RM for each exercise in Data table 1.0.

B. Measurement of Relative Muscular Endurance (RME)

1. Warm up with a weight that you can lift approximately 6-8 times. This serves as both a practice and a warm-up. Your partner spots the lift (if you have already completed the muscular strength (1 RM) assessment today, the warm-up is not needed).
2. Rest 2-4 minutes.
3. Set the load as close as possible to 60% of your 1 RM or use the percentage suggested by your instructor.
4. Using the lifting technique outlined in Box 1.0, complete as many repetitions as possible in 1 minute: Your partner spots the lift. You can rest with the weight in the up position, but the weight cannot be placed on the rack and then lifted off again.
5. Rotate stations and complete RME assessments for all muscle groups being investigated.
6. Record the number of repetitions performed for each exercise in Data table 1.0.

C. Measurement of Absolute Muscular Endurance (AME)

1. Warm up with a weight that you can lift approximately 10 times. This serves as both a practice and a warm-up. Your partner spots the lift (if you have already completed the muscular strength (1 RM) assessment today, the warm-up is not needed).
2. Rest for 2-4 minutes.
3. Set the load using Box 2.0 or use the load suggested by your instructor.
4. Using the technique outlined in Box 1.0, complete as many repetitions as possible in 1 minute: Your partner spots the lift. You can rest with the weight in the up position, but the weight cannot be placed on the rack and then lifted off again.
5. Rotate stations and complete AME assessments for all muscle groups being investigated.
6. Record the number of repetitions performed for each exercise in Data table 1.0.

Box 1.0
Procedures for Performing the Bench Press, Leg Press and Lat-Pull Down.

Bench Press

1. Assume a supine position on the bench with your eyes just under the front edge of the bar.
2. Grip the bar using a grip width a little wider than shoulder width (some people have difficulty balancing the bar if the grip width is too narrow).
3. With help from a spotter, raise the bar to a position directly over the shoulder joint.
4. In a controlled manner, lower the bar to the chest just below the inferior border of the pectoralis.
5. Pause for an instant (do not bounce the bar) and press the bar back up to full arm extension directly over the shoulder.

Leg Press

1. Sit in the seat with the hips pressed back against the pad as tightly as possible.
2. Place the feet flat on the platform approximately hip width apart and parallel or with toes pointed slightly outward.
3. The feet need to be placed high enough on the platform so that when the weight is lowered to the point where the thigh is perpendicular to the floor, the toes are even with or above the height of the knee.
4. With help from spotters, press the weight to full leg extension.
5. Lower the weight until the thigh is perpendicular to the floor.
6. Press the weight back up to full leg extension.

Lat-Pull

1. Sit erect, face the machine so that the front of the head is directly under the back edge of the bar.
2. Hold the hands up so the thumbs just touch the outside of the shoulder and reach straight up, grasping the bar with an over-hand grip that is slightly wider than shoulder width
3. Leaning back slightly (approximately 30° from upright), pull the bar down until it is below the chin with the head facing directly forward and not up. The bar should be pulled under control and not jerked down.
4. Lower the weight under control until the weight stack is down.

Box 2.0 Loads (lbs.) for Determining Absolute Muscular Endurance			
	Bench Press	Lat-Pull	Leg Press*
Men	80	75	225
Women	45	40	185

* *The load includes the plates and the weight of the sled.*

Data Table 1.0

Subject	Bench Press 1 RM*	Bench Press RME*	Bench Press AME*	Lat-Pull 1RM	Lat-Pull RME	Lat-Pull AME	Leg Press 1 RM	Leg Press RME	Leg Press AME
1									
2									
3									
4									
5									
6									
7									
8									
9									
10									
11									
12									
13									
14									
15									
16									
17									
18									
19									
20									
Mean									
SD									

* *1 RM, 1 Repetition Maximum. RME, Relative Muscular Endurance. AME, Absolute Muscular Endurance.*

Student Activities

A. Definitions.

Define the following key terms. For those terms which are measurable variables, describe in your own words what they mean (not how they are obtained or calculated). Indicate the unit(s) of measurement.

1. Absolute Muscular Endurance (AME):

2. Muscular Strength:

3. One Repetition Maximum (1 RM):

4. Relative Muscular Endurance (RME):

B. Analysis

1. Determine the relationship between muscular strength and RME. Your instructor may provide this statistical analysis.

2. Determine the relationship between muscular strength and AME. Your instructor may provide this statistical analysis.

3. Using the class data in Data Table 1.0, create two scattergrams and draw a line of best fit for a) the relationship between muscular strength (1 RM) and AME and b) the relationship between muscular strength (1 RM) and RME.

4. Evaluate your strength using the percentiles for strength for college age men or women in *Appendix A*.

C. Interpretation and Discussion.

1. Theoretically, what would you expect the relationship between muscular strength and RME to be? Explain why you expect this.

2. Theoretically, what would you expect the relationship between muscular strength and AME to be? Explain why you expect this.

3. Discuss the class results and draw conclusions.

4. Comment on your personal results.

D. Application.

1. How can this information be applied to assessment of muscular fitness?

2. Describe how an appropriate resistance training program to improve strength should vary from one designed to improve muscular endurance.

Related Readings

1. Plowman, S.A. & Smith, D.L. (2003). Exercise Physiology for Health, Fitness and Performance (2nd ed.). San Francisco: Benjamin Cummings.
2. Powers, S.K. & Howley, E.T. (2001). Exercise Physiology: Theory and Application to Fitness and Performance (4th ed.) (pp. 399-400). Boston: McGraw-Hill.
3. McArdle, W.D., Katch, F.I. & Katch, V.L. (2001). Exercise Physiology: Energy, Nutrition and Human Performance (5th ed.) (pp. 502-503, 506-507). Baltimore: Williams & Wilkins.

Muscular Fitness

Field Tests

Student Learning Objectives

After completing this lab, you should be able to:

1. Define, explain and correctly use key terms.
2. Distinguish between muscular strength, muscular endurance and muscular power.
3. Explain how to assess muscular strength, muscular endurance, muscular power, flexibility and balance using field tests.
4. Distinguish between relative and absolute muscular endurance.

Equipment

- Bench
- Cardboard Strips or Board (4.5 in wide/11.4 cm)
- Free Weights (2.5-25 lbs./1-12 kg)
- Goniometer
- Hand Grip Dynamometer
- Mats
- Measuring Tape/Ruler (12 inches/30.5 cm)
- Metronome/Stopwatches
- Pacing Tape/CD and Tape/CD Player (optional)
- Sit and Reach Box

Procedure

Muscular strength, muscular endurance, muscular power, flexibility and balance will be assessed using field tests. All students will be subjects; students should work with a partner and test each other. Begin with the balance test. Thereafter, proceed in any order, but complete all parts of each test before continuing on to the next one. Record your data in Data Table 1.0.

Protocols

A. <u>Balance Test: 1 Foot or "Stork" Stand</u>[2]

1. Remove your shoes and determine which foot will be the supporting foot.
2. Stand on the supporting foot and place the other foot flat against the inside of the supporting leg's knee. Place your hands on hips.
3. When instructed by your partner to begin, raise the heel of your supporting foot off the floor and balance for as long as possible without moving the supporting foot, touching the heel to the ground or removing your hands from hips.
4. Record the length of time proper balance is maintained (up to a maximum of 60 seconds) in Data Table 1.0 (to the nearest tenth of a second).
5. Perform one practice trial and two test trials. The best of the two test trials is taken as the final score.

B. <u>The Back Saver Sit and Reach</u>[1]

1. Remove your shoes and sit down at the sit and reach box.
2. Set the sit and reach box tape so that the level of the feet reads 9 inches (23 cm).
3. Fully extend one leg, with the foot flat against the end of the box. Bend the other knee, with the sole of the foot flat on the floor and 2-3 inches to the side of the extended knee. Sit with both hips square to the box.
4. Extend your arms forward over the measuring scale with the hands placed one on top of the other, palms down.
5. A partner makes sure that your extended knee

remains straight and that both hands remain together and in contact with the measuring tape

6. Reach forward with both hands along the scale four times and hold the position on the fourth reach for at least one second. If necessary, the bent knee may move to the side as the body bends forward.
7. A partner reads the point of furthest extension.
8. Repeat steps 2-7 using the opposite leg.
9. Record the distance (to the last whole inch or centimeter) in Data Table 1.0.

The test is repeated if:

- Your extended knee flexes (a partner may place one hand on your knee to remind you to keep the knee straight).
- Your hands do not reach forward evenly.
- Your hips do not remain square to the box.

C. Hand Grip

1. Adjust the dynamometer to fit your hand.
2. Perform a maximal contraction in a standing position, making sure that the test arm is neither touching any other body part, nor is in contact with any of your surroundings.
3. Perform 3 maximal contractions with the right and left hand, alternating hands to allow for a rest period.
4. Record grip strength (the highest of the 3 trials for each hand) in Data Table 1.0.

D. National Back Fitness Test (NBFT)[4]

Note to Student: This test should not be performed if you have had significant back problems, including surgery, in the past or if you are experiencing back pain at this time.

Three of the tests (the straight leg raise, sling test and lateral lift) require only one attempt. The fourth test (the sit-up) requires you to attempt successively easier versions of a sit-up if the proper form cannot be achieved. Place a check next to the grade of the exercise that you were able to complete correctly. The total score is the sum the grades on the individual tests.

(a) Straight Leg Raise Test

The goal of this test is to raise both legs simultaneously 6 inches off the floor for 10 seconds in the supine position. Terminate the test as soon as your lower back begins to curve away from the floor. A partner places his/her hand in the lordotic curve of your back to judge this. Begin each attempt with a pelvic tilt to flatten the back.

___**Grade 1**
Raised both legs 6 inches and held for 10 seconds while the back remained flat.

___**Grade 2**
Raised both legs 6 inches but back curved before 10 seconds elapsed.

___**Grade 3**
Raised both legs 6 inches, but back curved immediately.

___**Grade 4**
Unable to lift legs due to discomfort.

(b) Sling Test

The goal of this test is to maintain one leg straight, knee flat against the floor, while the other leg is flexed and pulled to the chest in a supine position. Test both the right and left leg. Average the scores if different scores are obtained for the right and left leg. A partner measures the distance between the straight leg knee and the floor.

___**Grade 1**
With one leg, held at the knee, pulled to the chest, the other leg remained flat on the floor.
Right: _____ Left: _____

___**Grade 2**
With one leg, held at the knee, pulled to the chest, the other knee was bent 2-4 inches off the floor.
Right: _____ Left: _____

___**Grade 3**
With one leg, held at the knee, pulled to the chest, the other knee was bent 4-8 inches off the floor.

Right: _____ Left: _____

___**Grade 4**
Could not get one leg to the chest without discomfort. The other leg was 8 inches or more off the floor.
Right: _____ Left: _____

(c) Lateral Lift Test

The goal of this test is to raise the shoulders and trunk laterally off the floor as far as possible without twisting the body either forward or backward. The starting body position is lying on your side with the legs straight, one on top of the other, and the arms folded across the chest. One partner is needed to stabilize the feet, while a second partner measures the height of the "down" shoulder above the ground. Average the scores if different scores are obtained for the right and left shoulder.

___**Grade 1**
Raised shoulder 12 inches off the floor without difficulty.
Right: _____ Left: _____

___**Grade 2**
Raised shoulder 6-12 inches off the floor, but it was difficult.
Right: _____ Left: _____

___**Grade 3**
Raised shoulders 2-6 inches off the floor, and it was difficult.
Right: _____ Left: _____

___**Grade 4**
Could not raise the shoulders off the floor.
Right: _____ Left: _____

(d) Sit-Up Test

The goal of this test is to complete a sit-up with proper form. This is the only one of the 4 tests which may require multiple trials. Begin with Grade 1. If the you cannot perform Grade 1, try Grade 2. If you cannot perform Grade 2, try Grade 3. Finally, if you cannot perform Grade 3, try Grade 4. If you are unable to perform the Grade 4 sit-up, record a score of 5. Make sure that your feet are free and not anchored or held in any way.

___**Grade 1**
Completed one sit-up with hands over ears, knees bent and feet flat on the floor.

___**Grade 2**
Completed one sit-up with arms crossed over chest, knees bent and feet flat on the floor.

___**Grade 3**
Completed one sit-up with arms held out straight in front of body, knees bent and feet flat on the floor.

___**Grade 4**
Completed one sit-up with arms held straight out in front of body and legs straight.

___**Grade 5**
Unable to complete any sit-up form.

E. <u>90° Push-Up.</u>[1]

1. Set a metronome to 40 beats·min^{-1}. Counting "push-up (1), lower-down (2)," each push-up takes 3 seconds.

> *<u>Note to Instructor</u>: A pre-recorded tape or CD, such as that provided with the FITNESSGRAM® Test Kit[1], may also be used; see Appendix B.*

2. Assume a prone position with the shoulders placed directly over the hands, arms fully extended, legs parallel, straight and slightly apart with the toes supporting the lower body.
3. Push up with your arms until fully extended, keeping both your legs and back straight.
4. Lower the body using your arms, keeping the back in a straight line from head to toes until the elbows reach 90° and the upper arms are parallel to the floor.
5. Maintain a controlled pace with the metronome of one push-up per 3 seconds until fatigue.
6. A partner checks to make sure that the 90° angle is achieved by placing his/her hand under your shoulder or chest at the appropriate height.
7. Count the number of push-ups performed and record in Data Table 1.0.

There is no time limit for the test, but the push-ups must be performed rythmically, correctly and continuously (to a maximum of 75). Terminate the test if:

- You experience severe discomfort or pain.
- You are unable to maintain a rythmic movement and must rest.
- You consistently display poor technique.

A partner attempts to correct your poor technique; however, if after 3 corrections you still display incorrect form, terminate the test. Poor technique is defined as:

- Knees touching the floor.
- Upper or lower back swaying.
- Failure to reach a complete arm extension.
- Failure to reach an approximate 90° bend at the elbow.
- The movement is too jerky.

F. Partial Curl-Up[1]

1. Make sure your feet are free and not anchored or held in any way.
2. Set a metronome to 40 beats·min^{-1}. Counting "curl-up (1), curl-down (2)," each partial curl takes 3 seconds.

> *Note to Instructor: A pre-recorded tape or CD, such as that provided with the FITNESSGRAM® Test Kit[1], may also be used; see Appendix B.*

3. Assume a supine position with the knees flexed to approximately 90-140° (a partner checks this angle between your thigh and lower leg with a goniometer), heels on the mat, arms extended on the floor parallel to the thigh, palms facing down.
4. Place your finger tips at the leading edge (edge closest to your buttocks) of a 4.5 inch piece of cardboard or on the platform of a curl-up tester.
5. Curl up (tilting the pelvis should be the first part of the motion) until your finger tips (sliding 4.5 inches) touch the end of the board or curl-up tester (angle of trunk ≤ 30°).
6. Return to the supine starting position.
7. Maintain a controlled pace with the metronome of one curl per 3 seconds until fatigue.
8. Count the number of partial curl-ups performed and record data in Data Table 1.0.

No pauses between curls are permitted, and your heels must remain in contact with the floor at all times. There is no time limit, but the test stops at a maximum of 75 curls. Terminate the test if:

- You experience severe discomfort or pain.
- You complete 75 correct partial curl-ups.
- You are unable to maintain correct rhythm for more than 3 repetitions and/or must rest.
- You consistently display poor technique.

A partner attempts to correct your poor technique; however, if after 3 corrections you still display incorrect form, terminate the test. Poor technique is defined as:

- Lifting the heels off the floor.
- Failure to slide the hands along the floor.
- Failure to slide the hands 4.5 inches along the floor.
- Failure to maintain knee angle.
- "Walking" of the buttocks.

G. Static Push-Up[3]

1. Assume a prone position with the shoulders placed directly over the hands, arms fully extended, legs parallel, straight and slightly apart with the toes supporting the lower body.
2. Lower your body by bending the elbows 90°, making sure your body is straight between the shoulders and toes.
3. A partner times how long you can maintain the 90° push-up position.
4. Terminate the test when you can no longer maintain the proper position (i.e., when the body is not maintained in a straight line between the shoulders and toes, or anything other than your hands or toes touch the floor).
5. Record the time in Data Table 1.0.

H. Trunk Extension Test[1]

1. Assume a prone position with your hands under

the thighs.

2. Using a slow, controlled motion, raise your head and upper body off the floor, making sure the pelvis maintains contact with the floor.
3. A partner measures the distance (to the nearest inch) from your chin to the floor using a tape measure.
4. Perform the test twice.

> *Note to Student: Heights greater than 12 inches/30.5 cm should not be encouraged.*

5. Record distance in Data Table 1.0.

I. Standing Long Jump[2]

1. Mark a take-off line on the floor using tape.
2. Position your toes close to, but not touching, the take-off line.
3. Jump as far forward as possible, making sure that both feet leave the ground simultaneously.
4. A partner measures the distance jumped (in inches) from the front of the take-off line to the back of the closest heel where landing contact was made.
5. Record distance in Data Table 1.0.

Data Table 1.0

Test	Score	Classification*	Healthy Fitness Criterion Achieved?*
Balance (s)			
Back Saver Sit and Reach (in/cm)			yes/no
Hand Grip (lbs./kg)			
Straight Leg Raise			
Sling			
Lateral Lift			
Sit-Up			
Total Score for NBFT			
90° Push-Up			
Partial Curl			yes/no
Static Push-Up			
Trunk Extension			yes/no
Standing Long Jump			

* *Note to Student: See Appendix A for classification based on gender.*

Student Activities

A. Definitions.

Define the following key terms. For those terms which are measurable variables, describe in your own words what they mean (not how they are obtained or calculated). Indicate the unit(s) of measurement.

1. Balance:

2. Flexibility:

3. Dynamic Absolute Muscular Endurance:

4. Dynamic Relative Muscular Endurance:

5. Power:

6. Static Absolute Muscular Endurance:

7. Static Relative Muscular Endurance:

8. Muscular Strength:

B. Analysis.

1. Based on the results of this lab, what is the level of your muscular fitness?

2. Match the fitness component generally measured with the field test item by placing a letter from Column II in front of Column I. Each letter from Column II may be used more than once, but Column I cannot have more than one letter. Note: Field tests are not always pure tests of fitness components.

Column I — Test Item:

___ 1. Hand Grip

___ 2. National Back Fitness Test

- ___ a. Lateral Raise
- ___ b. Sit-Up
- ___ c. Sling
- ___ d. Straight Leg Raise

___ 3. 90° Push-Up

___ 4. Partial Curl

___ 5. Sit and Reach

___ 6. Static Push-Up

___ 7. Trunk Extension

___ 8. Standing Long Jump

Column II — Fitness Components:

A. Balance

B. Flexibility

C. Dynamic Absolute Muscular Endurance

D. Dynamic Relative Muscular Endurance

E. Power

F. Static Absolute Muscular Endurance

G. Static Relative Muscular Endurance

H. Strength

3. Defend your matching of Column II to Column I in question 2.

C. Interpretation and Discussion.

1. What is the theoretical relationship between each of the items in the NBFT and back health?

D. Application.

1. Although all of these items would not normally be considered indicative of both health-related and sport-related physical fitness, suggest a situation in which each of the test items could be used to assess a) health-related fitness and b) sport-related fitness.

References

1. Cooper Institute for Aerobic Research (1992). FITNESSGRAM Test Administration Manual (2nd Ed.). Champaign, IL: Human Kinetics.
2. Hoeger, W.W.K. and Hoeger, S.A. (1999). Principles and Labs for Physical Fitness. Englewood, CO: Morton Publishing.
3. Hockey, R.V. (1981). Physical Fitness: the Pathway to Healthful Living (4th ed.). St. Louis: The C.V. Mosby Co.
4. Thygerson, A.L. (1989). Fitness and Health: Lifestyle Strategies. Boston: Jones & Bartlett Publishers.

Related Readings

1. Plowman, S.A. & Smith, D.L. (2003). Exercise Physiology for Health, Fitness and Performance (2nd ed.). San Francisco: Benjamin Cummings.
2. Powers, S.K. & Howley, E.T. (2001). Exercise Physiology: Theory and Application to Fitness and Performance (4th ed.) (414-416). Boston: McGraw-Hill.
3. McArdle, W.D., Katch, F.I. & Katch, V.L. (2001). Exercise Physiology: Energy, Nutrition and Human Performance (5th ed.) (pp. 501-507). Baltimore: Williams & Wilkins.

Flexibility

Static Stretching Versus PNF-CR

Student Learning Objectives

After completing this lab, you should be able to:

1. Define, explain and correctly use key terms.
2. Describe the acute effects of static stretching and proprioreceptive neuromuscular facilitation (PNF-CR) on joint range-of-motion (ROM).
3. Explain whether static stretching or PNF-CR increases joint ROM more.

Equipment

- Leighton Flexometer or Goniometer.

Procedure

The effect of two types of stretching on joint ROM will be examined: static stretching and PNF-CR. All students will be subjects; students should work with a partner and test each other.

Protocols

Warm up by walking or riding a cycle ergometer for 5 minutes.

A. Pre-Stretching ROM

1. Choose one leg to be stretched statically and the other to be stretched using PNF-CR.

> *Note: Alternate which leg is used for static stretching and which one for PNF-CR for every other participant.*

2. Utilizing a Leighton Flexometer or a goniometer, measure the passive flexibility of the hamstrings of each leg.
3. Record the ROM in Data Table 2.0 (Pre).

B. Static Stretching

1. Using the leg you chose for static stretching, stretch the hamstrings using the following two stretches: knee to chest and seated toe touch.
2. Hold each stretch for 30 seconds and perform each stretch twice.
3. After finishing the stretching routine, measure the passive flexibility of the hamstrings again (of the leg you just stretched statically).
4. Record the ROM in Data Table 1.0.

C. Proprioreceptive Neuromuscular Facilitation-Contract Relax (PNF-CR)

1. Lie on your back with both legs straight. Keeping the leg you stretched statically straight, raise your other leg as far as possible: Your partner should assist in pushing the hip into full flexion. Hold this position for 20 seconds.
2. Lower your leg back toward the floor about 5° and contract your leg extensors for 10 seconds: Your partner should resist the contraction.
3. After 10 seconds, relax your stretched leg and raise it again by active contraction as far as possible: Your partner should assist in pushing the leg into full flexion. Hold for 20 seconds.
4. From this "new" starting point, repeat steps 1 through 3 two more times.
5. Record the final ROM achieved in Data Table 1.0

Data Table 1.0

Subject	Static ROM (°)			PNF-CR ROM (°)		
	Pre	Post	Post - Pre	Pre	Post	Post - Pre
1						
2						
3						
4						
5						
6						
7						
8						
9						
10						
11						
12						
13						
14						
15						
16						
17						
18						
19						
20						
Mean						
SD						

Student Activities

A. Definitions.

Define the following key terms. For those terms which are measurable variables, describe in your own words what they mean (not how they are obtained or calculated). Indicate the unit(s) of measurement.

1. Flexibility:

2. Proprioreceptive Neuromuscular Facilitation-Contract Relax (PNF-CR):

3. Range-of-Motion (ROM):

4. Static Stretching:

B. Analysis

1. Prepare a bar graph of pre and post ROM values for both static and PNF-CR stretching.

2. Analyze the mean differences between pre and post ROM for PNF-CR and static stretching in Data Table 1.0 using a dependent t-test. Your instructor may provide the statistics.

C. Interpretation and Discussion.

1. Describe and discuss the results of the statistical analysis.

2. Describe, compare and contrast your personal results with the mean results from the statistical analysis.

3. Describe the proprioceptive basis for PNF-CR stretching.

D. Application.

1. In a flexibility training program, is it better to use static stretching or PNF-CR stretching? Support your answer.

2. Defend or Refute: Stretching for the improvement of ROM should occur at the end of a work-out when the muscles are "warm."

Related Readings

1. Plowman, S.A. & Smith, D.L. (2003). Exercise Physiology for Health, Fitness and Performance (2nd ed.). San Francisco: Benjamin Cummings.
2. Powers, S.K. & Howley, E.T. (2001). Exercise Physiology: Theory and Application to Fitness and Performance (4th ed.) (p. 419). Boston: McGraw-Hill.

Muscular Soreness

Immediate Versus Delayed Onset

Student Learning Objectives

After completing this lab, you should be able to:

1. Define, explain and correctly use key terms.
2. Distinguish between immediate muscle soreness and delayed onset muscle soreness (DOMS).
3. Describe the time course for the onset of, and reduction in, DOMS.
4. Explain which type of activities are most likely to cause DOMS.
5. Describe the effects of DOMS on muscle force production.
6. Evaluate the role of lactic acid/lactate in immediate and DOMS.

Equipment

- Dumbells (5-75 lbs./2-35 kg)
- Lactate Analyzer and Accessories
- Metronome

Procedure

The effects of muscle soreness on muscle force production will be examined. For this lab, students must work in pairs; for each pair of students, one student will be an *experimental* subject and one will be a *control* subject.

<u>Note to Instructor</u>: *This lab will take two separate days, that should be no more than 72 hours apart, to complete. Measurement of blood lactate concentration is optional.*

Protocols

A. <u>Day 1—Blood Lactate Measurements *(Control and Experimental Subjects)*</u>

1. Obtain a resting blood lactate measurement from

all subjects and record in Data Table 1.0 (Pre).

B. <u>Day 1—Determination of 1 Repetition Maximum (1 RM) (*Control* and *Experimental* Subjects)</u>

1. Determine the maximal amount of weight that can be lifted with the dominant arm (concentric 1 RM).
2. Stand with your back braced against a wall and perform 1 repetition of a biceps curl, ***lifting the weight only***.
3. Add weight until the weight can no longer be lifted with proper form 1 time. At that point, rate your *Magnitude of Muscular Distress (MOMD)* for the maximal lift using the pain scale in Box 1.0.
4. Record your MOMD and 1 RM (Pre Concentric) in Data Table 1.0.
5. Determine the maximal amount of weight that can be lowered using the non-dominant arm (eccentric 1 RM).
6. Stand with your back braced against a wall and perform 1 repetition of a biceps curl, ***lowering the weight only***.
7. Begin with the concentric 1 RM weight; add or subtract weight as necessary until the weight can no longer be lowered in a controlled manner. At that point, rate your MOMD for the maximal lift using the pain scale in Box 1.0.

8. Record your MOMD and 1 RM (Pre Eccentric) in Data Table 1.0.

C. Day 1—Determination of Muscular Endurance *(Experimental Subjects)*

1. Calculate 60% of your 1 RM.
2. Set the metronome to 60 beats·min^{-1} and stand with your back braced against a wall.
3. Lift the 60% 1 RM with the dominant arm (biceps curl) and lower it with the non-dominant arm (reverse biceps curl) until exhaustion in the following manner:

   - **Count 1**
     Weight in dominant hand, flex both arms.
   - **Count 2**
     Transfer weight from dominant hand to non-dominant hand.
   - **Count 3**
     Weight in non-dominant hand, extend both arms.
   - **Count 4**
     Transfer weight from non-dominant hand to dominant hand.

4. If the muscular endurance test exceeds five minutes, terminate the test and add more weight for the second bout of endurance activity. Record the weight used and the time to exhaustion in Data Table 1.0.
5. Rest for 5 minutes.
6. Repeat step 3. Immediately upon cessation of the second bout of endurance exercise, record the weight used and the time to exhaustion in Data Table 1.0, and record your MOMD for **both** arms (concentric and eccentric) in Data Table 2.0 (immediate post-exercise: IM Post).
7. Continue to record your MOMD for 72 hours.

> *Note: The control subject does no activity during this time; however, he/she should record his/her MOMD in Data Table 3.0 after the experimental subject's second bout of endurance exercise (IM Post) as well as for the next 72 hours.*

D. Day 1—Blood Lactate Measurements *(Control and Experimental Subjects)*

1. Obtain blood lactate values from both the control and experimental subjects after the experimental subject has completed the endurance exercise. Do control subjects immediately and experimental subjects 3 minutes post-exercise and record in Data Table 1.0 (Post).

E. Day 1—Strength Post-Test *(Control and Experimental Subjects)*.

1. Re-test concentric and eccentric 1 RM and record in Data Table 1.0 (Post Concentric and Post Eccentric).

F. Day 2—Blood Lactate Measurements *(Control and Experimental Subjects)*

1. Obtain a resting blood lactate value from all subjects and record in Data Table 1.0 (Day 2, Pre).

G. Day 2—Determination of 1 RM *(Control and Experimental Subjects)*.

1. Determine your concentric and eccentric 1 RM and record in Data Table 1.0.

Box 1.0
Magnitude of Muscular Distress[1] (MOMD)
1 No pain. 2 Dull, vague ache apparent upon touch. 3 Slight persistent pain exaggerated with use. 4 Painful: Interferes with use. 5 Very Painful: Avoid using. 6 Unbearably painful: Can't use.

Data Table 1.0							
	Experimental Subject				Control Subject		
Day 1	Time to Exhaustion	Weight (lbs./kg)	Pain (MOMD)	Lactate ($mmol \cdot L^{-1}$)	Weight (lbs./kg)	Pain (MOMD)	Lactate ($mmol \cdot L^{-1}$)
Pre							
Pre Concentric 1 RM							
Post Concentric 1 RM							
Pre Eccentric 1 RM							
Post Eccentric 1 RM							
Muscular Endurance Test 1							
Muscular Endurance Test 2							
Post							
Day 2							
Pre							
Concentric 1 RM							
Eccentric 1 RM							

Box 1.0
Magnitude of Muscular Distress[1] (MOMD)
1 No pain. 2 Dull, vague ache apparent upon touch. 3 Slight persistent pain exaggerated with use. 4 Painful: Interferes with use. 5 Very Painful: Avoid using. 6 Unbearably painful: Can't use.

Data Table 2.0

Experimental Subject

Distress Rating Concentric Arm	0	.25	.5	.75	1				2				3				4				5				6
IM post																									
12 hours																									
24 hours																									
48 hours																									
72 hours																									
Distress Rating Eccentric Arm	0	.25	.5	.75	1				2				3				4				5				6
IM post																									
12 hours																									
24 hours																									
48 hours																									
72 hours																									

Data Table 3.0

Control Subject

Distress Rating Concentric Arm	0	.25	.5	.75	1				2				3				4				5				6
IM post																									
12 hours																									
24 hours																									
48 hours																									
72 hours																									
Distress Rating Eccentric Arm	0	.25	.5	.75	1				2				3				4				5				6
IM post																									
12 hours																									
24 hours																									
48 hours																									
72 hours																									

Student Activities

A. Definitions.

Define the following key terms. For those terms which are measurable variables, describe in your own words what they mean (not how they are obtained or calculated). Indicate the unit(s) of measurement.

1. Concentric Contraction:

2. Delayed Onset Muscle Soreness (DOMS):

3. Eccentric Contraction:

4. Fatigue:

5. Immediate Muscle Soreness:

6. One Repetition Maximum (1 RM):

B. Analysis.

1. Prepare a bar graph illustrating the change in 1 RM pre-post for both the experimental and control subject on Day 1.

2. Prepare a bar graph illustrating the change in 1 RM Day 1 pre to Day 2 for both the experimental and control subject.

3. Prepare a line graph indicating the degree of muscle soreness for concentric and eccentric arms over the past 72 hours for both the experimental and control subject.

4. Prepare a bar graph illustrating lactate values Day 1 (pre and post) to Day 2 (pre) for both the experimental and control subject.

C. Interpretation and Discussion.

1. Discuss the results of the Day 1 pre-post 1 RM bar graph, draw conclusions from the results and physiologically explain the results.

2. Discuss the results of the Day 1 versus Day 2 1 RM bar graph, draw conclusions from the results and physiologically explain the results.

3. Discuss the results of the degree of muscle soreness graph, draw conclusions from the results and physiologically explain the results.

4. Discuss the results of the lactate bar graph, draw conclusions from the results and physiologically explain the results.

5. Differentiate between immediate and DOMS. Discuss the physiological cause(s) for immediate soreness. Discuss and evaluate at least two referenced theories for the physiological causes of DOMS.

D. Application.

1. Name five (5) sport or exercise activities that are likely to cause DOMS. Defend your selections.

2. Name five (5) sport or exercise activities that are not likely to cause DOMS. Defend your selections.

Reference

1. Talag, T.S. (1973). Residual muscular soreness as influenced by concentric, eccentric and static contractions. Research Quarterly for Exercise and Sport, 44 (4), 458-469.

Related Readings

1. Plowman, S.A. & Smith, D.L. (2003). Exercise Physiology for Health, Fitness and Performance (2nd ed.). California: Benjamin Cummings.
2. Powers, S.K. & Howley, E.T. (2001). Exercise Physiology: Theory and Application to Fitness and Performance (4th ed.) (pp. 417-418). Boston: McGraw-Hill.
3. McArdle, W.D., Katch, F.I. & Katch, V.L. (2001). Exercise Physiology: Energy, Nutrition and Human Performance (5th ed.) (pp. 540-543). Baltimore: Williams & Wilkins.

Appendix A

Physical Fitness Profile Charts For College Age Males

Classification	National Back Fitness Test	Systolic BP (mmHg)	Diastolic BP (mmHg)	Max VO_2 PACER Step Test ($mL \cdot kg^{-1} \cdot min^{-1}$)	Peak Power WAT (watts)	Peak Power ($watts \cdot kg^{-1}$)	Mean Power WAT (watts)	Mean Power ($watts \cdot kg^{-1}$)	Fatigue Index % WAT	Static Push-Up (s)	AnP Step Test (watts)
Reference#	15	14	14	4	12	12	12	12	12	7	1
Excellent	4 5	94 102 110	60 64	≥60	867 822	11.08 10.89	677 662	8.63 8.24	21 23	114 111	730 608 584
Very Good		112 116	70 72	52-59	807 777 768	10.59 10.39 10.39	631 618 604	8.09 8.01 7.96	27 29 30	106	554 536 520
Good	6 7 8	118	78	43-51	757 744 721	10.20 10.00 9.80	600 592 577	7.91 7.70 7.59	31 34 35	102 100	507 495 483
Average		120	80	42	706 689 678	9.51 9.22 9.02	575 565 553	7.46 7.44 7.26	37 38 39	97	472 460 448
Fair	9 10	128 130	84	34-41	671 662 656	8.92 8.63 8.53	548 535 530	7.14 7.08 7.00	40 42 44	94 92	438 425 413
Poor		132 136	88	25-33	646 618 594	8.34 8.24 7.45	521 496 485	6.79 6.59 6.39	45 46 47	88	400 384 360
Very Poor	11 12	140 150 158	90 100 110	≤24	570 531	7.06 6.57	471 453	5.98 5.56	52 55	83 80	336 312

Classification	HW or Skinfold (% BF)	90° Push-Ups (reps)	Vertical Jump (in)	Agility Run (s)	Grip Strength Right (lbs)	Grip Strength Left (lbs)	Standing Long Jump (cm)	Balance (s)
Reference#	10, 13	11	5	5	5	5	8	8
Excellent	5	61 53	28 27 26	12.8 13.7 14.6	184 177 171	170 164 157	>94	59.8 46.9 41.1
Very Good	8	50 48 43	25 24 23	15.4 16.3 17.2	164 158 151	151 145 139		24.9
Good	10	40 36	22 21 20	18.1 19.0 19.8	145 138 132	133 127 121	90-94	15.4 12.0
Average	13 15	34 33 31	18 17 16	20.7 21.6 22.5	125 118 112	115 109 102	85-89	9.2
Fair	17	30 28	15 14 13	23.4 24.2 25.1	105 99 92	96 90 84	77-84	7.3 5.8
Poor	18 22	25 24 22	12 11 10	26.0 26.9 27.8	86 79 73	78 72 66	76	4.3
Very Poor	25	20 16	9 7 6	28.6 29.5 30.4	66 60 53	60 54 48	<76	3.1 2.6

Physical Fitness Profile Charts For College Age Females

Classification	National Back Fitness Test	Systolic BP (mmHg)	Diastolic BP (mmHg)	Max VO_2 PACER Step Test ($ml \cdot kg^{-1} \cdot min^{-1}$)	Peak Power WAT (watts)	Peak Power ($watts \cdot kg^{-1}$)	Mean Power WAT (watts)	Mean Power ($watts \cdot kg^{-1}$)	Fatigue Index % WAT	Static Push-Up (s)	AnP Step Test (watts)
Reference#	15	14	14	4	12	12	12	12	12	7	1
Excellent	4 5	90 98	56 60 64	≥55	602 560	9.32 9.02	483 470	7.52 7.31	20 25	38 35	490 407 391
Very Good		100	68	48-54	530 527 518	8.92 8.83 8.63	437 420 414	7.08 6.95 6.93	25 26 28	32	370 358 348
Good	6 7 8	106 110	70 72	38-47	505 493 480	8.53 8.34 8.14	410 402 391	6.77 6.65 6.59	29 30 33	30 28	339 331 322
Average		112	74 76	37	464 449 447	7.85 7.65 7.16	386 381 377	6.51 6.39 6.20	34 35 37	26	315 307 299
Fair	9 10	118 120	78 80	31-36	433 418 399	6.96 6.96 6.86	367 361 353	6.15 6.13 6.03	38 39 40	24 22	292 283 275
Poor		122	80	24-30	396 376 362	6.77 6.57 6.37	347 337 320	5.94 5.71 5.56	42 43 44	20	266 258 244
Very Poor	11 12	130 140	82 88 90	≤23	353 330	5.98 5.69	306 287	5.25 5.07	47 48	17 14	223 207

Classification	HW or Skinfold (% BF)	90° Push-Ups (reps)	Vertical Jump (in)	Agility Run (s)	Grip Strength Right (lbs)	Grip Strength Left (lbs)	Standing Long Jump (cm)	Balance (s)
Reference#	10, 13	11	5	5	5	5	8	8
Excellent	16	40 26	18 17	15.9 16.6 17.3	106.5 102 98	99 95 91	>74	59.9 39.1 25.8
Very Good	18	23 20 17	16 15	18.0 18.8 19.5	93 89 85	87 83 79		16.7
Good	20	15	14 13	20.2 20.9 21.7	81 77 73	75 71 67	70-74	11.9 9.8
Average	25	13 12 11	12 11	22.4 23.1 23.8	69 65 60	63 59 55	64-69	7.6
Fair	28	10 9	10 9 8	24.6 25.3 26.0	56 52 48	50 46 42	58-63	6.2 5.0
Poor	32	6 5 4	7 6	26.8 27.5 28.2	44 40 36	38 34 30	57	4.2
Very Poor	39	3 2	5 4	28.9 29.6 30.4	32 27 23	26 22 18	<57	2.9 1.8

Norms Table for Criterion - Referenced Tests[3]				
Criterion-Referenced Classification	Trunk Extension (inches)	Back Saver Sit and Reach (inches)	Partial Curl (# of Reps)	Body Mass Index (BMI) ($Kg \cdot m^{-2}$)
Healthy Fitness	12 - 9	≥ 12 Females ≥ 8 Males	18-35 Females 24-47 Males	18-27.3 Females 19 - 27.8 Males
Needs Improvement	8 or less	< 12 Females < 8 Males	< 18 Females < 24 Males	> 27.4 Females > 27.9 Males
Reprinted with permission from the Cooper Institute for Aerobics Research, Dallas, TX.				

Percentiles for Strength for College Age Males and Females [2,6,9]						
	Males			Females		
Percentile	Bench Press*	Lat-Pull*	Leg Press*	Bench Press	Lat-Pull*	Leg Press*
99	300	270	940		145	530
95	238	230	815		130	470
90	225	225	770		125	440
85	215	220	730		120	420
80	205	215	710		115	400
75	200	210	690		110	390
70	195	210	665		105	375
65	190	200	640		100	370
60	190	200	635		100	360
55	185	195	630		100	345
50	180	190	615		95	330
45	175	190	600		95	325
40	170	190	570		90	320
35	165	185	560		85	310
30	157	180	545		85	300
25	155	180	540		80	290
20	150	175	515		80	280
15	145	170	500		75	260
10	135	160	475		70	250
5	125	150	435		65	240
1	100	130	350		60	220
* *1 RM scores are in pounds.*						

References

1. Adams, G.M. (1994). Exercise Physiology Laboratory Manual (2nd ed.) (p. 76). Dubuque, IA: Wm C. Brown.
2. Ball, T.E., VanFleet, R.J., Lahey, R.J. & Glass, L.A. (1995). The relationship of relative muscular endurance to maximal lifting capacity in college men and women. Journal of Strength and Conditioning Research, 9 (4), 277.
3. Cooper Institute for Aerobics Research (1999). FITNESSGRAM Test Administration Manual (2nd ed.) (pp. 38-39). Champaign, IL: Human Kinetics.
4. Cooper, K.H. (1970). The New Aerobics (pp. 28-31: modified). New York: Bantam Books.
5. Cureton, T.K. (1970). Physical Fitness Workbook for Adults (pp. 120, 216: Modified). Champaign, IL: Stipes Publishing Co.
6. Druffel, K. (1995). Absolute muscular endurance as a predictor of leg extension lifting ability in college women. Unpublished Master's thesis. Northern Illinois University, DeKalb, IL.
7. Hockey, R.V. (1981). Physical Fitness: The Pathway to Healthful Living (4th ed.) (pp. 62, 65). St. Louis: The C.V. Mosby Co.
8. Hoeger, W.W.K. & Hoeger, S.A. (1997). Principles and Labs for Physical Fitness (p. 189). Englewood, CA: Morton Publishing Co.
9. Invergo, J.I., Ball, T.E. & Looney, M (1991). Relationship of push-ups and absolute muscular endurance to maximal bench press strength. The Journal of Applied Sport Science Research, 5 (3), 121-125.
10. Lohman, T.G., Houtkooper, L. & Going, S.B. (1997). Body Fat Measurment Goes High-Tech. ACSM's Health and Fitness Journal, 1 (1), 30-35.
11. Massicote, D. (1990). Partial curl-ups, push-ups and multi-stage 20 meter shuttle run, national norms for 6-17 year olds. Final report to: Canadian Association for Health, Physical Education and Recreation (CAHPER) and Fitness and Amateur Sport Canada (pp. 43, 44). University of Quebec, Montreal.
12. Maud, P.J. & Schultz, B.B. (1989). Norms for the Wingate Anaerobic Test with Comparison to Another Similar Test. Research Quarterly for Exercise and Sport, 60 (2), 144-151(modified).
13. Plowman, S.A. & Smith, D.L. (2003). Exercise Physiology for Health, Fitness and Performance (2nd ed.)(p. 363). San Francisco: Benjamin Cummings.
14. Pollock, M.L., Wilmore, J.H. & Fox, S.M. (1989). Health and Fitness Through Physical Actvity (pp. 266-267, 276-277: modified). Santa Barbara, CA: John Wiley & Sons.
15. Thygerson, A.L. (1989). Fitness and Health: Life-Style Strategies (p. 140). Boston: Jones & Bartlett Publishers.

Appendix B

Addresses

1. PACER and cadence tapes for curl-ups and 90° push-ups.

   American Fitness Alliance
   Human Kinetics
   P.O. Box 5076
   Champaign, IL 61825-5076
   www.americanfitness.net/Fitnessgram/
   Fitnessgram Kit
   1.800.747.4457

2. Chicken Fat: The Youth Fitness Video.

   Chicken Fat Enterprises
   P.O. Box 687
   Aberdeen, N.J. 07747

Journals in Exercise Science and Physiology

1. ACSM's Health and Fitness Journal
2. American Journal of Sports Medicine
3. Archives of Physical Medicine and Rehabilitation
4. Athletic Therapy Today
5. Aviation, Space and Environmental Medicine
6. Canadian Journal of Applied Physiology
7. Canadian Journal of Sport Sciences
8. European Journal of Applied Physiology
9. Exercise Immunology Review
10. Human Biology
11. International Journal of Sports Medicine
12. International Journal of Sports Nutrition
13. Journal of Aging and Physical Activity
14. Journal of Applied Biomechanics
15. Journal of Applied Physiology
16. Journal of Applied Sport Science Research
17. Journal of Biomechanics
18. Journal of Gerontology
19. Journal of Human Movement Studies
20. Journal of Neurophysiology
21. Journal of Orthopedic and Sports Physical Therapy
22. Journal of Osteopathic Sports Medicine
23. Journal of Physiology
24. Journal of Sports Medicine and Physical Fitness
25. Journal of Sports Rehabilitation
26. Journal of Sports Sciences
27. Journal of the American Medical Association
28. Medicine and Science in Sport and Exercise
29. Metabolism Research
30. Journal of Strength and Conditioning Research
31. Pediatric Exercise Science
32. Pflugers Archives
33. Physical Therapy
34. Physician and Sports Medicine
35. Research Quarterly for Exercise and Sport
36. Respiration Physiology
37. Scandinavain Journal of Sport Sciences
38. Sports Medicine
39. Strength and Conditioning

Selected Reading List

1. Alter, M.J. (1996). Science of Flexibility (2nd ed.). Champaign, IL: Human Kinetics.
2. American College of Sports Medicine (1999). Guidelines for Exercise Testing and Prescription.(6th ed.) Philadelphia, PA: Lea & Febiger.
3. American College of Sports Medicine (2001). Resource Manual for Guidelines for Exercise Testing and Prescription (4th ed.). Philidelphia, PA: Lippincott, Williams & Wilkins.
4. Anschel, M.H. (ed.), Freedson, P. Hamill, J., Haywood, K., Horvat, M. & Plowman, S.A. (1991). Dictionary of Sport and Exercise Sciences. Champaign, IL: Human Kinetics.
5. Armstrong, L.E. (2000). Performing in Extreme Environments. Champaign, IL: Human Kinetics.
6. Astrand, P.O. & Rodahl, K. (1989). Textbook of Work Physiology (4th ed.). New York: McGraw Hill.
7. Baechle, T.R. & Earle, R. (eds.) (2000) National Strength and Conditioning Association (2000). Essentials of Strength Training and Conditioning (2nd ed.). Champaign, IL: Human Kinetics.
8. Bar-Or, O. (1983). Pediatric Sports Medicine for the Practitioner. New York: Springer-Verlag.
9. Bompa, T.O. (1999). Periodization: Theory and Methodology of Training (4th ed.). Champaign, IL: Human Kinetics.
10. Borg, G. (1998). Borg's Perceived Exertion and Pain Scales. Champaign, IL: Human Kinetics.
11. Bouchard, C., Shephard, R.J. & Stephens, T. (eds.) (1994). Physical Actvity, Fitness and Health. Champaign, IL: Human Kinetics.
12. Brooks, G.A., Fahey, T.D., White, T.P. & Baldwin, K.M. (2000). Exercise Physiology: Human Bioenergetics and its Application (3rd ed.). Mountain View, CA: Mayfield Publishing Co.
13. Caillet, R. (1988). Low Back Pain Syndrome. Philadelphia, PA: F.A. Davis Co.
14. DeVries, H.A. & Housch, T.J. (1994). Physiology of Exercise for Physical Education and Athletics (5th ed.). Dubuque, IA: Wm. C. Brown.
15. Fleck, S.J. & Kramer, W.J. (1997). Designing Resistance Training Programs (2nd ed.). Champaign, IL: Human Kinetics.
16. Foss, M.L. & Keteyian, S.J. (1998). Fox's Physiological Basis for Exercise and Sport (6th ed.). Boston: McGraw Hill.
17. Hasson, S.M. (1993). Clinical Exercise Physiology. St. Louis: Mosby.
18. Heyward, V.H. (1998). Advanced Fitness Assessment and Exercise Prescription (3rd ed.). Champaign, IL: Human Kinetics.
19. Heyward, V.H. & Stolarczyk, L.M. (1996). Applied Body Composition Assessment. Champaign, IL: Human Kinetics.
20. Hochschuler, S.H. (1990). The Spine in Sports. St. Louis: Mosby-Yearbook.
21. Howley, E.T. & Franks, B.D. (1997). Health Fitness Instructor's Handbook. Champaign, IL: Human Kinetics.
22. MacDougall, J.D., Wenger, H.A. & Green, H.J. (eds.) (1991). Physiological Testing of the Elite Athlete (2nd ed.). Champaign, IL: Human Kinetics.
23. McArdle, W.D., Katch, F.L. & Katch, V.L. (1996). Exercise Physiology: Energy, Nutrition and Human Performance (5th ed.). Baltimore: Williams & Wilkins.
24. McArdle, W.D., Katch, F.I. & Katch, V.L. (1999). Sport and Exercise Nutrition. Philadelphia: Lippincott, Williams & Wilkins.
25. Malina, R.M. & Bouchard, C. (1991). Growth, Maturation and Physical Activity. Champaign, IL: Human Kinetics.
26. Pangrazi, R.P. & Corbin, C.B. (1994). Teaching Strategies for Improving Youth Fitness (2nd ed.). Reston, VA: American Alliance for Health, Physical Education, Recreation and Dance.

27. Plowman, S.A. & Smith, D.L. (2003). Exercise Physiology for Fitness, Health and Performance (2nd ed). San Fransisco: Benjamin Cummings.
28. Powers, S.K. & Howley, E.T. (2001). Exercise Physiology (4th ed.). Boston: McGraw Hill.
29. Strand, B.N., Scantling, E. & Johnson, M. (1997). Fitness Education: Teaching Concepts-Based Fitness in the Schools. Scottsdale, AZ: Gorsuch Scarisbrick Publishers.
30. Robergs, R.A. & Roberts, S.O. (1997). Exercise Physiology: Exercise, Performance and Clinical Applications. St. Louis: Mosby.
31. Rowland, T.W. (1996). Developmental Exercise Physiology. Champaign, IL: Human Kinetics.
32. Wells, C.L. (1991). Women, Sport and Performance: A Physiological Perspective (2nd ed.). Champaign, IL: Human Kinetics.
33. Weltman, A. (1995). The Blood Lactate Response to Exercise. Champaign, IL: Human Kinetics.
34. Wilmore, J. & Costill, D.L. (1996). Physiology of Sport and Exercise (2nd ed.). Champaign, IL: Human Kinetics.
35. Zatsiosky, V.M. (1995). Science and Practice of Strength Training. Champaign, IL: Human Kinetics.

Appendix C

24 Hour Inventory

Name: ____ Date: __________ Time: __________ a.m./p.m.
Last First MI

Instructions: Make sure to fill in each item. Use an X to indicate appropriate items.

General Condition:

Cold: _______ Headache: _______ Muscle Soreness: _______
Nasal Congestion: _______ Sore Throat: _______ Other: _______
Intestinal Disorder: _______ Digestive Upset: _______

How do you feel? Good: _______ Fair (average): Not so Good: _______ Bad: _______

If not so good, or bad, specify: ____

Rest:

Sleep Last Night: Time to Bed (a.m./p.m.): _______ Time Arising (a.m./p.m.): _______ No. Hours: _______
Quality of Sleep: Sound: _______ Awakened Once: _______ Restless, Frequently Awake: _______
Bed rest Today: Yes: _______ No: _______ If yes, time to bed: _____ Time Up: _______ No. Hours: _______

Food Intake:

Last meal: Time Starting: _______ a.m./p.m. Time ending: _______ a.m./p.m.

Kind of Food	Amount of Food	Kind of Food	Amount of Food

Food and Liquid Intake Since last Meal:

Kind	Amount	Time

Alcohol:

Kind	Amount	Time

Medicine and Drugs — Indicate medicines taken in the past 24 hours:

Kind	Amount	Time

Physical Activity — Has your physical activity pattern over the past 24 hours been:

Very Vigorous: _____ Vigorous: _____ Moderate: _____ Mild: _____ Very Mild: _____

Give further details indicating the kinds of activity engaged in over the past 24 hours:

Kind and Length of Time	Time of Day

Appendix D

Physical Fitness Lesson Plan

Throughout the term, you will devise three (3) separate lesson plans either for students in a school physical education setting (if you are working toward teacher certification or coaching) or adult fitness/rehabilitation setting (if you are an exercise science, sport medicine or sport management degree candidate). One topic will fall into the broad category of cardiovascular-respiratory exercise physiology, a second will be metabolic exercise physiology and the third will be neuromuscular physiology. The order of the categories will be determined by your instructor.

Place a 1, 2 or 3 in front of the following components of exercise physiology to indicate the order in which your lesson plans are to be completed.

_______ a. Cardiovascular-Respiratory Fitness

_______ b. Metabolic Fitness

_______ c. Neuromuscular Fitness

The possible topics within each area of exercise physiology are as follows. Circle your choice in each area.

Note to Instructor: Topics may, of course, be added or deleted. Students may self-select, draw lots for or be assigned topics. The topics are intentionally broad to allow students to exhibit creatvity and variation.

A. Cardiovascular-Respiratory Fitness

1. exercise and the heart
2. what heart rate and blood pressure responses to exercise are "normal"
3. using heart rate for exercise prescription
4. cardiovascular-respiratory exercise myths
5. the Valsalva maneuver
6. respiration and exercise
7. cardiovascular endurance/fitness
8. exercise in the heat
9. cardiovascular disease/risk factors
10. maximal oxygen consumption

B. Metabolic Fitness

1. energy systems
2. aerobic versus anaerobic energy and activities
3. lactic acid/lactate
4. energy expenditure/caloric cost
5. body composition and weight control
6. eating disorders
7. exercise and metabolism myths
8. electrolyte drinks, gels and energy bars
9. ergogenic aids—the good, the bad and the worthless

C. Neuromusculo-Skeletal Fitness.

1. agility
2. balance
3. flexibility
4. muscular strength, endurance and power
5. injury prevention
6. exercise and neuromuscular myths
7. osteoporosis/risk factors
8. building muscle for fitness
9. low back health
10. delayed onset muscle soreness

Lesson Plan

1. Title, grade level and time. Pedagogy students may select any grade level (K-6th = elementary; 7th-9th = junior high school; 10th-12th = senior high school). Non-teaching degree students may select young adult (18-40yr), middle-aged adult (40-60yr) or older adult (>60yr). Elementary and junior high school, select 20-30 minutes for the period; high school and adult, select a 45-60 minute period. Indicate your choice. Be specific (e.g., "Lesson Title," 4th Graders, 20 minute period).

2. Analysis and description of setting. Complete the following information.

   a. Previous physical fitness training experience of the class members. Where does this specific lesson fit in? (day number X in unit out of X number of total days)

   b. Available facilities and equipment needed for this lesson.

   c. Class size and composition.

   d. Lesson objectives. These should be as specific as possible. Include both psychomotor (physical activity) and cognitive (knowledge of basic concepts) objectives.

e. For each objective listed in 2d, indicate specifically how you are going to evaluate whether that objective was achieved or not.

f. How will individual differences be accomodated in each part of this lesson?

g. The relationship between the physical activity portion of the lesson and/or its relevancy to your cognitive topic.

3. Lesson plan. Complete the attached *Lesson Plan Form*. Additional pages may be added as needed. Provide all the information that would be needed for someone else to teach this class if you were not present.

Lesson Plan Form				
Time	Teaching/Learning Objectives	Teacher/Student Organization	Description of Activities	What to Look For/ Cues/ Feedback

Physical Fitness Unit Plan

Note to Instructor: This may be done as separate units to allow feedback and correction, or it may be completed and handed in all at once.

Throughout the term, you will develop a total physical fitness unit plan either for students in a school setting (if you are working toward teacher certification or coaching) or adults in a health club/fitness setting (if you are an exercise science, sports medicine or sport management degree candidate). The unit plan will be completed in three parts in the order specified by your instructor. For example, you might be assigned the order, cardiovascular-respiratory fitness, metabolic fitness and neuromuscular fitness. In this sequence, you would concentrate first on developing cardiovascular-respiratory fitness; all activities and concepts should relate only to the cardiovascular-respiratory systems. The second part of this sequence would integrate the development of metabolic fitness with your cardiovascular-respiratory component. In the third part of this sequence, you would integrate neuromuscular fitness development into what you have already done for cardiovascular-respiratory fitness and metabolic fitness.

Place a 1, 2 or 3 in front of the following components of exercise physiology to indicate the order in which your unit assignments are to be completed.

_______ a. Cardiovascular-Respiratory Fitness

_______ b. Metabolic Fitness

_______ c. Neuromuscular Fitness

If you select an elementary or junior high school grade:

1. You will complete two, 3-week physical fitness units: One for September, when outdoor space is available and can be used, and the other for February, when only indoor space is available.
2. The class meets 5 days per week for 30 minutes each day.
3. Each class period is to be divided as follows:
   a. Introductory Activity (warm-up) — 3-5 minutes
   b. Lesson Focus: Fitness Development (main activities) — 20-24 minutes
   c. Closing Activity (cool-down) — 3-5 minutes
   d. Cognitive Understanding (may be integrated in any of the three phases, but must be integrated regularly)
4. You must select a variety of activities (choose at least 3 endurance actvities for cardiovascualr-respiratory development and 3 muscular for neuromuscular fitness. Metabolic actvities may overlap cardiovascular-respiratory actvities), and they must be different for each 3 week unit. For example, if you use calisthenics in the fall, you cannot repeat this type of activity in the spring.

If you select a senior high school grade or adult population:

1. You will complete one, 6-week physical fitness unit plan.
2. The class meets 5 days per week for 45 minutes of activity each day.
3. Each actvity period is to be divided as follows:
   a. Warm-up — 5-10 minutes
   b. Main Body of Actvity — 30-40 minutes
   c. Cool-Down — 5-10 minutes

d. Cognitive Understanding (may be integrated in any of the three phases, but must be integrated regularly)

4. You must select one core aerobic actvity and one cross-training aerobic actvity. The neuromuscular modality may be the same for the entire unit.

Unit Plan

1. Title and grade level. Pedagogy students may select any grade (K-6th = elementary; 7th-9th = junior high school; 10th-12th = senior high school). Non-teaching degree students may select young adult (18-40 yr), middle-aged adult (40-60 yr) or older adult (>60 yr). Indicate your choice.

2. Analysis and description of setting. Complete the following information.

   a. Previous physical fitness training experience of the class members.

   b. Available facilities and equipment for unit(s).

   c. Class size and composition.

   d. Basic organization of the class (i.e., attendance procedure grouping of participants, role of teacher/ fitness leader, method of orientation to new actvities, etc.).

   e. Objectives. These should be as specific as possible. They must be relevant, measurable and realistically achievable. Include both psychomotor (physical actvity) and cognitive (knowledge of basic concepts) objectives.

3. Scientific basis of unit. Answer the following questions.

a. How will overload be achieved at the beginning of each activity in the unit?

b. How will adaptation be determined? Describe any assessment tools and how they will be used. Provide any record keeping sheets or simulation of computer print-outs that will be used by the instructor or class members.

c. How will progression be accomplished?

d. How will individualization be taken into account for overload, adaptation and progression?

4. Block Schedule. Complete the attached *Unit Plan Block Calendar* for the unit. You may need to xerox extra copies before completing the schedule. Keep in mind that you are going to build a complete unit. For example, you may wish to work on cardiovascular-respiratory fitness each day or only on certain days. State which you are going to do and why. Remember, later you will be adding activities specific for metabolic fitness and finally for neuromuscular fitness benefit. Of course, you may be starting with neuromuscular fitness, but the idea is to allow for the integration of all three components of fitness within your plan. Include the amount of time devoted to each actvity. For activities that are not readily identifiable, place an asteric (*) by the name and attach a how-to description that someone not familiar with the activity could easily follow.

Unit Plan Block Calendar

	Monday	Tuesday	Wednesday	Thursday	Friday
Introductory Activity Main Activities Closing Activity					
Introductory Activity Main Activities Closing Activity					
Introductory Activity Main Activities Closing Activity					

Sport Specific Exercise Prescription

Throughout the term, you will be analyzing a particular fitness activity, sport, event or position within a sport and developing a series of exercise prescriptions.

Note to Instructor: Students may be permitted to select a fitness activity, sport, event or position, or they may draw one by a lot. A partial list of possibilities is given on the last page of this project.

Indicate the activity that you have selected:____

1. Analyze your activity for each of the following physiological fitness components. Do so by listing as many skills that depend upon that physiological component as possible and/or providing numerical values for individuals trained in that activity.

   Aerobic Power (VO_2 max):

   Anaerobic Power:

   Anaerobic Capacity:

   Body Composition:

   Agility:

   Balance:

   Flexibility:

   Muscular Endurance:

   Muscular Power:

   Strength:

   Other Components (name each):

2. Complete the *Specificity of Exercise Prescription Chart* based on the analysis you just completed. Assume this is for pre-season for an athletic sport or a previously sedentary individual for a fitness activity. The exercise prescription should incorporate individualization. Be sure to cover the major fitness components for as many parts of the body as possible, but emphasize just the major skills. Note: The exercise prescription is not intended to be done on one day. Presented below are partial examples for two diverse sports: Volleyball (spike) and 5000 meter run (last 800 m).

Specificity of Exercise Prescription Chart (Example*)

Skill/Body Characteristics	Fitness Component	Training Activity	Exercise Prescription	Evaluation Technique
volleyball spike	muscular power legs	plyometrics	sets = 2/session reps = 12/set exercises: split squat jump squat jump double-leg zig zag hop depth jumps (.3-.5 m box) sets = 2/session reps = 12/set exercises: medicine ball push-ups	completion of the sets and reps with effort
	arms	weight training	sets = 2/session reps = 12-15 RMs/set speed = fast positive phase exercises: bent arm pullover lying triceps extension lat pull-down seated dumbell press	
5000 m (last 800 m)	anaerobic capacity	intervals	sets = 1 of each reps = 4 x 400 m and 2 x 800 m speed = [1600 m ÷ 4] - 1 to 4 s/400m [1600 m ÷ 4] + 3 to 4 s/800m	lactate > 4mM RPE 17-20
	muscular power	plyometrics	sets = 2/session reps = 10/set exercises: 1 legged hops 2 legged hops depth jumps	completion of the sets and reps with effort

* *Note to Student: Continue the chart as needed to be comprehensive for your activity.*

3. Give a brief description of each exercise used or include an illustration. For example, Split Squat Jump: The individual starts in a lunge position, one leg in front of the body, the other behind with both feet pointed forward; the individual jumps into the air, switches leg positions and lands in the lunge position. Attach additional pages as needed.

List of Sports/Events

Aerobic dance	Hammer Throw	Rugby
Badminton	Handball	Sailing
Baseball	High Jump	Shot Put
Basketball	Horseback Riding	Skateboarding
Cowboy Line Dancing	Ice Hockey	Softball
Cross-Counry Skiing (distance)	Indoor Soccer	Speed Skating
Cycling (distance: $\geq$ 20 km)	Inline Skating	Squash
Cycling (sprint)	Javelin	Surfing
Discus	Karate	Swimming:
Diving	Kayaking	50 meter
Downhill Skiing	Lacrosse	100-200 meter
Fencing	Long Jump	500-800 meter
Field Hockey	Mountain Biking	1500 meter
Figure Skating	Olympic Lifting	Synchronized
Football:	Powerlifting	Track:
Defensive Backs	Soccer (non-goalie)	< 200 m sprints/hurdles
Linemen	Tennis	400-800 m sprints/hurdles
Offensive Backs	Racquetball	1500 m - 5 km
Quarterbacks	Rock Climbing	marathon (42 km)
Receivers	Rodeo	Triple Jump
Golf	Rollerblading	Water Polo
Gymnastics:	Rowing:	Wrestling
Men's	2000 meters	
Women's	3.5 miles	

Specificity of Exercise Prescription Chart				
Skill/Body Characteristics	Fitness Component	Training Activity	Exercise Prescription (intensity and duration only)	Evaluation Technique for Overload Achievement

Periodization of Training Plan

Throughout the term, you will develop a periodization plan either for yourself or for one of the fictional individuals described later. Periodization is the structured sequential development of physiological fitness and athletic skill with the intent of peaking an individual for competion by organizing training into set blocks of time and closely monitoring the individual to determine adaptation.

Note to Instructor: This project can be done in stages (cardiovascular-respiratory periodization, metabolic periodization and neuromuscular periodization in any order) or completed all at the same time.

If you are developing a periodization plan for yourself, complete the following table:

Name: ____________________								
Sport or Fitness Activity	*Age*	*Sex*	*Height*	*Weight*	*VO_2 max ($mL \cdot kg \cdot min^{-1}$)*	*Resting HR ($b \cdot min^{-1}$)*	*Maximal HR ($b \cdot min^{-1}$)*	*% BF*

- Current Training: ____
- Relevant Performances (personal records within the past 3 months and date each was done): ____________________
- Goal (one year away): ____

If you are not developing a periodization plan for yourself, select one of the following fictional individuals (exercise science, sports medicine, sport management or other non-teaching degree majors should select either Drew or Lisa and teacher education majors or coaching majors/minors should select either Emily or Kyle).

Drew							
Sport	*Age*	*Sex*	*Height*	*Weight*	*VO_2 max*	*Resting HR*	*% BF*
Fitness Runner	32	male	5'8"	185 lbs.	45 $mL \cdot kg \cdot min^{-1}$	72 $b \cdot min^{-1}$	21%

- Current Training: Runs 3 days/week, 3-5 miles/day at a conversational pace.
- Personal Record: 60:38 for 10 km race - set today.
- Goal: 48:00 for next year's 10 km race.

Lisa							
Sport	*Age*	*Sex*	*Height*	*Weight*	*VO_2 max*	*Resting HR*	*% BF*
Recreational Cyclist	40	female	5'8"	145 lbs.	40 $mL \cdot kg \cdot min^{-1}$	84 $b \cdot min^{-1}$	21%

- Current Training: Rides 2 days/week indoors for 45 minutes and 10-30 miles outdoors (weather permitting) on Saturday and Sunday.
- Personal Record: 7 hours and 30 minutes for a century (100 mile) bike ride - set yesterday.
- Goal: 6 hours and 15 minutes for next year's century.

Emily							
Sport	*Age*	*Sex*	*Height*	*Weight*	*VO_2 max*	*Resting HR*	*%BF*
High School Volleyball Player	16	female	6'0"	152 lbs.	38 ml·kg·min^{-1}	74 b·min^{-1}	17%

- Current Training: Practices or plays 5-6 days/week 2 hours/day during the season. During the summer, she plays softball 2 nights/week.
- Team Record: 3rd in Conference Championships.
- Team Goal: Conference and State Championship next year.
- Personal Goal: Increase vertical jump by 7-10 cm; increase velocity of spike; increase power output.

Kyle							
Sport	*Age*	*Sex*	*Height*	*Weight*	*VO_2 max*	*Resting HR*	*%BF*
1500 m Swimmer	15	male	5'6"	118 lbs.	50 ml·kg·min^{-1}	58 b·min^{-1}	10%

- Current Training: Swims 5-6 days/week 2 hours/day in practice or meets; generally does the front crawl all that time.
- Personal Record: 18:14 for 1500 m - set today at the Conference meet.
- Goal: 16:00 for 1500 m.

Periodization Plan

1. Using the individual you selected, prepare a physiological profile of successful (elite) athletes of the same sex and sport. Give specific numerical values.

   a. Cardiovascular Variables:

   b. Metabolic Variables:

   c. Neuromuscular Variables:

2. Using the physiological profile values as goals, describe the changes you wish to achieve to give your selected individual a reasonable chance of reaching his/her goal.

3. Describe how and when you are going to monitor these physiological and performance goals for your selected individual. What signs or symptoms of overtraining will you look for?

4. Determine the number of weeks in the following year that will be devoted to the macrocycles of transition phase (active rest), general preparatory phase (off-season training), specific preparatory phase (pre-season training) and competitive phase (in-season training—early and late). Show that division proportionally on the following circle, and label it appropriately. Justify your time decisions.

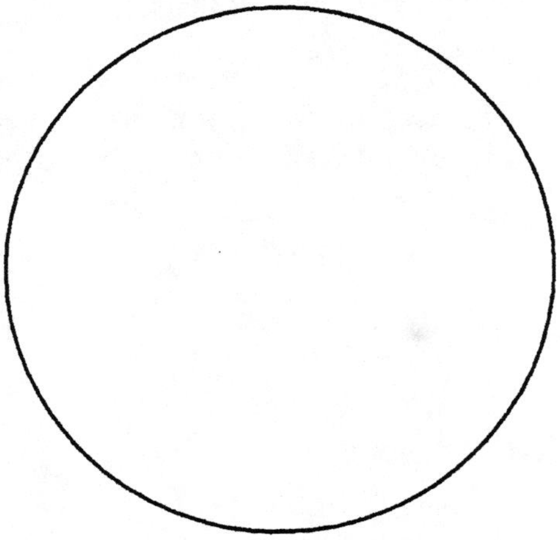

5. Complete the *Periodization Chart*. Place this month at the extreme left and proceed through the year. Plot the percentage of time or effort that is to be devoted to each of the following components throughout the year.

   a. Training Volume (total time spent in training)
   b. Training Intensity (cardiovascular and metabolic)
   c. Resistance Training (volume and intensity)
   d. Sport Technique

   For example, if rowing were the sport, the sport technique line in the *Periodization Chart* might look as follows:

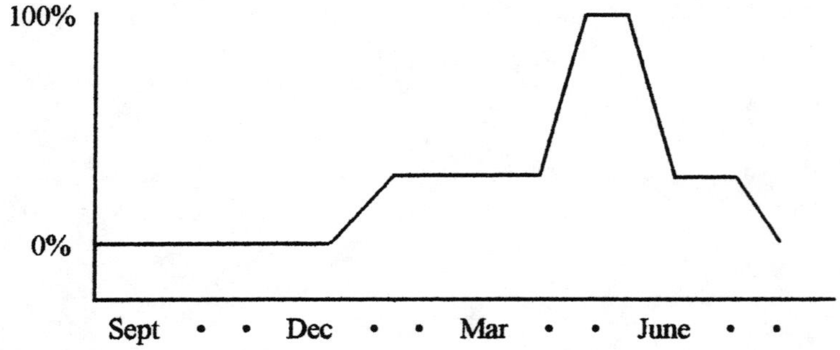

   In this case, September to December corresponds to transition phase (active rest) and early general preparation phase (off-season), December through March to late general preparation phase (off-season) and specific preparatory phase (pre-season) and June through August to early and late competitive phase (in-season).

   Your graph will have four lines on it, not just one, as indicated above (i.e., one for each of the 4 components listed above). Scientifically defend your percentages and pattern.

6. Your macrocycles may or may not be the same length. However, within a macrocycle, each single week is called a microcycle. Four microcycles are sometimes termed a mezocycle. Select one mezocycle from the pre-season macrocycle and show how you would vary each of the four training components (training volume, training intensity, resistance training and sport technique). This should be a bar graph presentation using the chart labeled *Pre-Season Mezocycle*.

   For example, if rowing were the sport, the bars for technique work in the *Pre-season Mezocycle Chart* might look as follows:

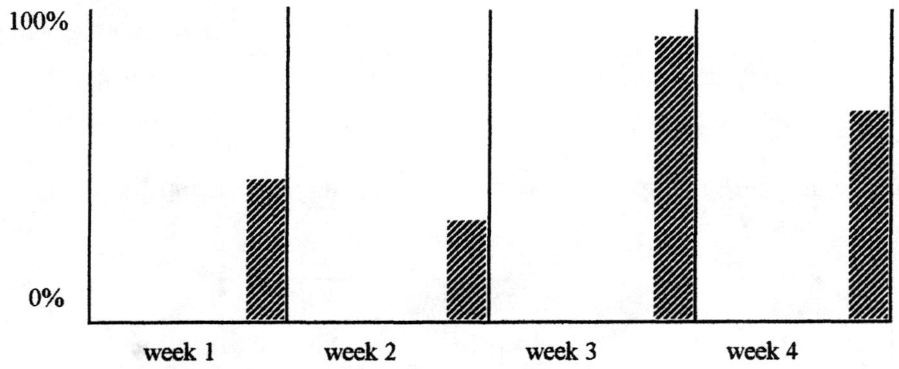

   Your graph will have four bars per week, one for each of the listed training components. Identify the primary goal or pattern for this mezocycle (developmental, shock, maintenance, tapering or unloading, transition or regeneration). Scientifically defend your percentages and pattern.

7. Using the following activities, or adding others of the same general nature, plan one microcycle from within your specific preparatory phase (pre-season) mezocycle using the chart labeled *Pre-Season Microcycle*. Briefly describe the workout in terms of overload (i.e., distance and heart rate, lactate level or sets, reps and load, etc.).

Aerobic Intervals	Plyometrics
Anaerobic Intervals	Rest
Continuous Aerobic Endurance Workout	Resistance Training
Cross-Training Activties	Sport Technique/Drills
Fartlek Training	Static/Dynamic Calisthenics
Isokinetic Training	Team Play
Lactate Threshold Training	Tempo Runs

For example, if rowing were the sport, a day from the microcycle during the competitive phase might look as follows:

Monday	
A.M.	*Aerobic Endurance Workout (Continuous):* 1 hour at a heart rate of 148-160 $b \cdot min^{-1}$
P.M.	*High Intensity Anaerobic Training:* 15 sets of 15 strokes at 95% effort

Identify the primary goal or pattern for this microcycle (developmental, shock, maintenance, tapering or unloading, transition or regeneration). Scientifically defend your percentages and pattern.

Periodization Chart

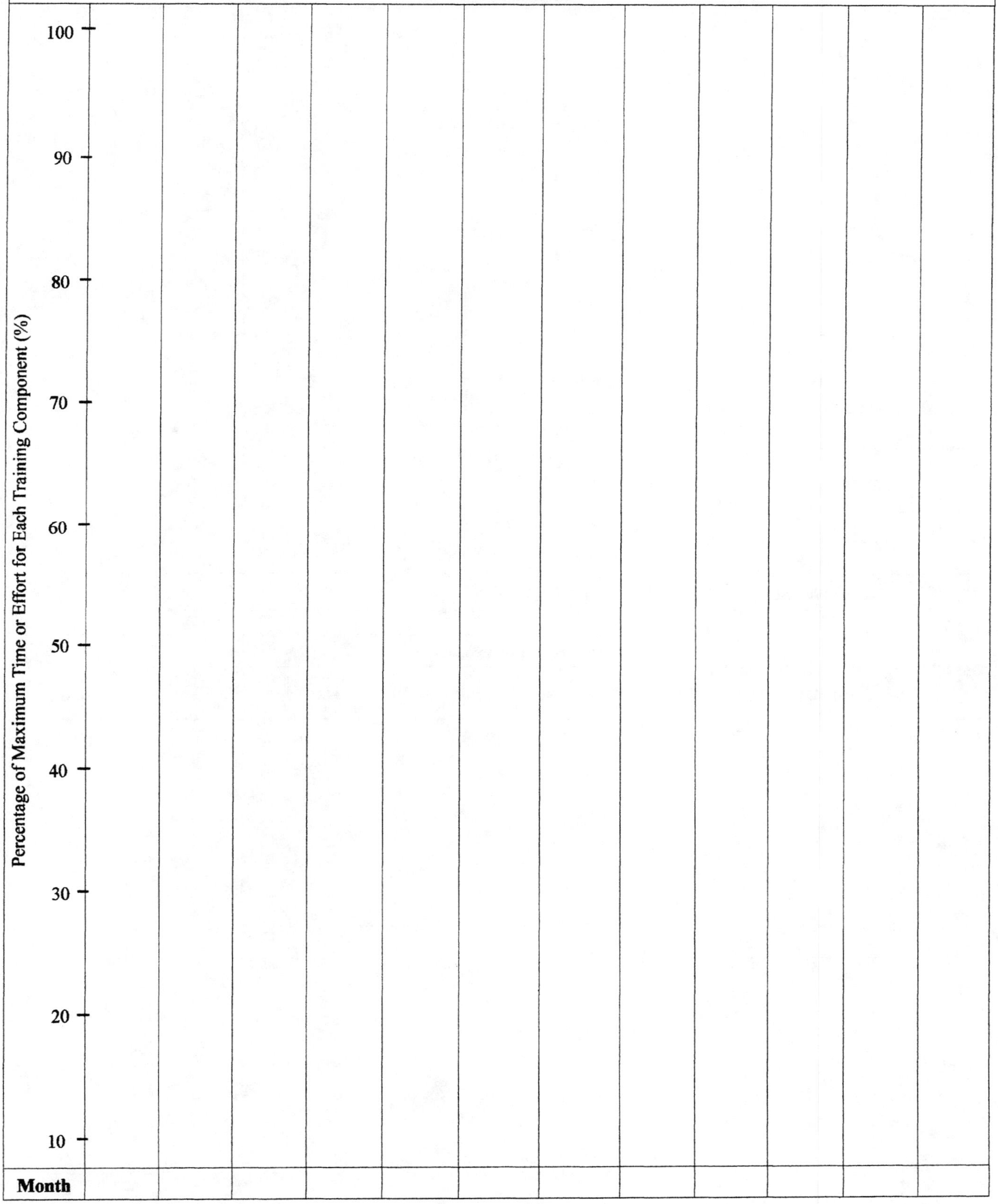

Pre-Season Mezocycle

Percentage of Maximum Time or Effort for each Training Component (%)				
100				
90				
80				
70				
60				
50				
40				
30				
20				
10				
	Week 1	Week 2	Week 3	Week 4

Pre-Season Microcycle

	Monday	Tuesday	Wednesday	Thursday	Friday	Saturday	Sunday
A.M.							
P.M.							

Experimental Training Adaptations

During this term, you will develop and evaluate a training program for yourself. Data collection and training session cooperation will be determined by your instructor.

A. Pre-Testing

1. Perform the five protocols representing the different categories of exercise as described in the *Responses to Different Categories of Exercise* lab.

2. Select one field test that allows an estimation of VO_2 max, one that tests dynamic muscular strength or endurance, and any other field test that you are interested in and perform those tests according to the instructions in the appropriate lab. List the field tests you have selected in the following table:

	Field Test		
Estimated VO_2 max			
	Muscle Group	Strength	Endurance
Muscular Strength or Endurance	____________ ____________ ____________	____________ ____________ ____________	____________ ____________ ____________
Other			

B. Training

1. On the basis of your results, plan and execute a 3-6 week training program. Treat this time span as if it were a mezocycle and plot the variations in training frequency, duration and intensity for both cardiorespiratory-metabolic activities and resistance training activities using the chart labeled *Training Overload Plan*.

   For example, in a 6 week program, the line for frequency for resistance training might look as follows:

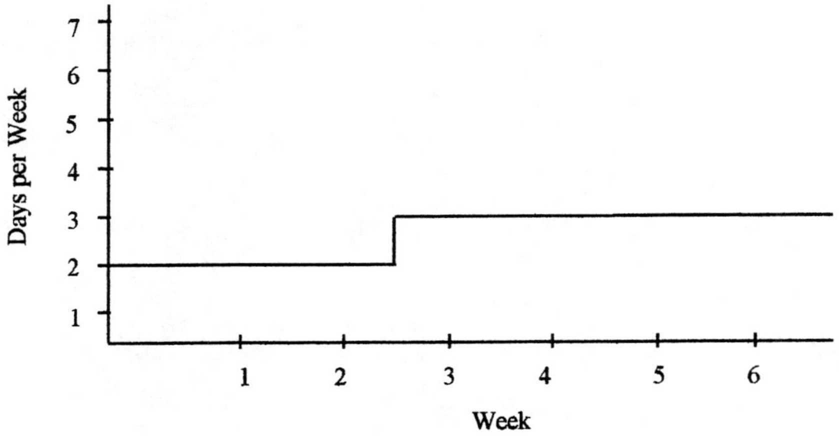

2. On the basis of your overall plan, write out your exercise prescriptions week by week on the chart labeled *Weekly Training Plan and Log*. Keep an accurate and honest log of what you actually did during each planned exercise session on the same form. Adjust the following week's exercise plan on the basis of what you have actually done to that time. You should xerox extra copies of the *Weekly Training Plan and Log* before beginning.

C. Post-Testing

1. Repeat all of the pre-tests.
2. Write your final report to include the following sections:
   a. Introduction
   b. Method
   c. Results (including tables and graphs)
   d. Discussion of the Results
   e. Conclusions and Recommendations
   f. "What I Learned From This Project"

Weekly Training Plan and Log

	Planned Exercise Prescription	Accomplished Exercises
Sunday		
Saturday		
Friday		
Thursday		
Wednesday		
Tuesday		
Monday		

Training Overload Plan

Percent Intensity	Duration (minutes)	Frequency (total workouts/week)	Week 1	Week 2	Week 3	Week 4	Week 5	Week 6
100	100	10						
90	90	9						
80	80	8						
70	70	7						
60	60	6						
50	50	5						
40	40	4						
30	30	3						
20	20	2						
10	10	1						

Evaluation of Articles in Popular Magazines

Throughout the term, you will be evaluating articles published in magazines intended for the general public. You may be asked to find the articles or your instructor may provide them for you. Complete each evaluation as follows:

1. Write a brief summary of the article you have been given or chosen. In your summary, be sure to identify the main point of the article and any conclusions. Also, in three or more sentences, explain how this article relates to class and, more specifically, to the lab. Finally, give some practical application of the information in the article.

2. Find a research study that either supports or refutes the main point of the article you have been given (you do not need to limit your study to the same exercise modality as that discussed in the article) and write an abstract (a brief summary of 150-200 words) of it. You should find a research study* presented in a journal like Research Quarterly for Exercise and Sport, Medicine and Science in Sport and Exercise or Journal of Stength Conditioning Research, but not Ironman, Muscle Media, Training and Conditioning or other magazines of this type written for the general public.

* *Note to Student: A research study is one in which the authors ask some question, recruit subjects to study, collect data on the subjects, analyze the data and talk about what they have found.*

The abstract should include the following:

A. Reference at the Top. Use a complete reference including the authors (last name and initials of each author), article and journal title and publication information (i.e., year, volume and pages).
B. Purpose of the Study
C. Methodology
   - Subjects: Tell who the subjects were (e.g., young adult men with weight training experience).
   - What was measured? List the variables measured and briefly explain testing procedures.
   - Experimental manipulation, if any (e.g., subjects were given creatine monohydrate).
   - Statistical Analysis
D. Results
   - Give mean values and identify if any differences were statistically significant. Don't just write that group one increased strength and group two increased endurance, tell by how much; for example, group one increased strength by 27 pounds or 15%.
E. Conclusions
   - What did the study show? Note: Results are not the same as conclusions.

3. Explain how this article refutes or supports the main point of the article that you were given or selected. Don't write, "The research supports the main idea in my article." Tell explicitly how the research supports the article. If the research refutes the article, write a paragraph correcting the information in the article. If the research supports the article, write a paragraph extending the article.

4. Indicate how this reading relates to other things you have read or discussed in this or other classes. Think about this and give more than just one sentence. Do not write that you don't know anything about this topic.

5. Give at least one practical application of this information. How can this information be used?

Exercise Advice Column

Throughout the term, you will be answering questions such as you might get from individuals wishing to take advantage of your expertise.

<u>Note to Instructor</u>: These questions may be real ones you have received, ones printed in publications such as <u>Runner's World</u>, <u>Triathlete</u>, <u>Bike</u>, <u>ACSM's Health and Fitness Journal</u>, etc., or fabricated to empahsize certain key concepts.

Complete each question as follows:

1. Answer the question by providing sound, scientifically based advice, giving very specific and accurate information. If the question allows for different interpretations, give these possibilities and answer accordingly. You should always attempt to go beyond the question to provide information about safety concerns, appropriate methods of training, etc. Your answer should be in language the general public can understand, but it must be scientifically based. While advice columns do not typically reference the answers, you must do so.

2. Find a research study that supports your answer and write an abstract (a brief summary of 150-200 words) of it. The abstract should include the following:

   A. Reference at the Top. Use a complete reference including the authors (last name and initials of each author), article and journal title and publication information (i.e., year, volume and pages).
   B. Purpose of the Study
   C. Methodology
      - Subjects: Tell who the subjects were (e.g., young adult men with weight training experience).
      - What was measured? List the variables measured and briefly explain testing procedures.
      - Experimental manipulation, if any (e.g., subjects were given creatine monohydrate).
      - Statistical Analysis
   D. Results
      - Give mean values and identify if any differences were statistically significant. Don't just write that group one increased strength and group two increased endurance, tell by how much; for example, group one increased strength by 27 pounds or 15%.
   E. Conclusions
      - What did the study show? Note: Results are not the same as conclusions.

3. Explain how this article refutes or supports the main point of your advice. Don't write, "The research supports my advice." Tell explicitly how the research supports your advice.